Navigating Colour-Blind Societies

Navigating Colour-Blind Societies is a comparative ethnography of racialisation class, and gender in the lives of young Muslims coming of age in societies, where race is deemed insignificant.

The book offers insights into the urban lives of young middle-class Muslims in Copenhagen and Montreal. Based on their narratives, the book examines racialisation as (1) a social process that is classed and gendered and (2) a spatial process that is social and temporal. Denmark and Quebec have seen an increasing thrust of nationalist politics in recent years, which position their Muslim citizens as the quintessential "Other." The book contributes to our understanding of how Muslims are racialised and how they navigate this process of racialisation in social and urban life. The interaction between movement and life stories provides a unique vantage point in bringing the city to life from the perspective of these young adults.

The book appeals widely to academics and students in sociology, anthropology, and human geography. It also appeals to a wider audience interested in anti-racist scholarship and Muslim experiences in the Global North.

Amani Hassani is a Leverhulme Early Career Fellow at Brunel University. She is an urban ethnographer working at the intersection of sociology, anthropology, and human geography. Her research explores the connection between racialisation and spatialisation, focusing on Muslim populations in the Global North. She has written widely on racialisation, Islamophobia, and Muslim experiences in academic and public domains.

Routledge Advances in Ethnography

Edited by Dick Hobbs, University of Essex and Les Back, Goldsmiths, University of London

Ethnography is a celebrated, if contested, research methodology that offers unprecedented access to people's intimate lives, their often hidden social worlds and the meanings they attach to these. The intensity of ethnographic fieldwork often makes considerable personal and emotional demands on the researcher, while the final product is a vivid human document with personal resonance impossible to recreate by the application of any other social science methodology. This series aims to highlight the best, most innovative ethnographic work available from both new and established scholars.

The Logic of Violence
An Ethnography of Dublin's Illegal Drug Trade
Brendan Marsh

Black Men in Britain
An Ethnographic Portrait of the Post-Windrush Generation
Kenny Monrose

Moving Difference
Brazilians in London
Angelo Martins Junior

Selling the Kimono
An Ethnography of Crisis, Creativity and Hope
Julie Valk

Fighting Identity
An Ethnography of Kickboxing in East London
Amit Singh

Navigating Colour-Blind Societies
A Comparative Ethnography of Muslim Urban Life in Copenhagen and Montreal
Amani Hassani

For more information about series page, please visit https://www.routledge.com/Routledge-Advances-in-Ethnography/book-series/RETH.

Navigating Colour-Blind Societies
A Comparative Ethnography of Muslim Urban Life in Copenhagen and Montreal

Amani Hassani

LONDON AND NEW YORK

Designed cover image: © Amani Hassani

First published 2024
by Routledge
4 Park Square, Milton Park, Abingdon, Oxon OX14 4RN

and by Routledge
605 Third Avenue, New York, NY 10158

Routledge is an imprint of the Taylor & Francis Group, an informa business

© 2024 Amani Hassani

The right of Amani Hassani to be identified as author of this work has been asserted in accordance with sections 77 and 78 of the Copyright, Designs and Patents Act 1988.

All rights reserved. No part of this book may be reprinted or reproduced or utilised in any form or by any electronic, mechanical, or other means, now known or hereafter invented, including photocopying and recording, or in any information storage or retrieval system, without permission in writing from the publishers.

Trademark notice: Product or corporate names may be trademarks or registered trademarks, and are used only for identification and explanation without intent to infringe.

British Library Cataloguing-in-Publication Data
A catalogue record for this book is available from the British Library

Library of Congress Cataloging-in-Publication Data
Names: Hassani, Amani, author.
Title: Navigating colour-blind societies: a comparative ethnography of Muslim urban life in Copenhagen and Montreal / Amani Hassani.
Other titles: Navigating color-blind societies
Description: Abingdon, Oxon; New York, NY: Routledge, 2024. |
Series: Routledge advances in ethnography | Includes bibliographical references and index.
Identifiers: LCCN 2023041315 (print) | LCCN 2023041316 (ebook) |
ISBN 9781032279268 (hbk) | ISBN 9781032279299 (pbk) | ISBN 9781003294696 (ebk)
Subjects: LCSH: Muslim youth–Québec (Province)–Montréal–Social conditions. |
Muslim youth–Denmark–Copenhagen–Social conditions. | Muslims–Québec (Province)–Montréal–Social conditions. | Muslims–Denmark–Copenhagen–Social conditions. |
Islamophobia–Québec (Province)–Montréal. | Islamophobia–Denmark–Copenhagen. |
Montréal (Québec)–Ethnic relations. | Copenhagen (Denmark)–Ethnic relations.
Classification: LCC F1054.5.M89 M885 2024 (print) | LCC F1054.5.M89 (ebook) |
DDC 971.4/270088297--dc23/eng/20231010
LC record available at https://lccn.loc.gov/2023041315LC ebook record available at https://lccn.loc.gov/2023041316

ISBN: 978-1-032-27926-8 (hbk)
ISBN: 978-1-032-27929-9 (pbk)
ISBN: 978-1-003-29469-6 (ebk)

DOI: 10.4324/9781003294696

Typeset in Sabon
by Deanta Global Publishing Services, Chennai, India

For Aya, Yaqeen, and Ameen.

Contents

List of Figures		*viii*
Acknowledgements		*x*
Introduction: Muslims in Colour-Blind Societies		1
PART I		
Muslim Racialisation and its Affects		**21**
1	Assemblages of Muslim Racialisation	23
2	Middle-Class Muslim Respectability in Copenhagen	36
3	Gendered Islamophobia, Representation, and the Hijab in Montreal	58
PART II		
Muslim Pathways and Spatial Narratives		**75**
4	Contesting Racialised Spaces in Copenhagen	77
5	Spatial Biographies and Rootedness in Montreal	105
6	Space, Time, and the Urban Muslim	134
Conclusion: Navigating Colour-Blind Societies		148
References		*153*
Index		*160*

Figures

1.1 "Church. Synagogue. Mosque. Sacred—Equality between men and women. The State's religious neutrality. All also sacred."—Parti Quebecois (provincial government party in Quebec in 2013). National campaign billboard at a metro-station in downtown Montreal, advocating "The Charter of Values" (Bill 60) banning "ostentatious" religious symbols in public spaces   31

1.2 "Stop Nazi Islam ism"—Conservative People's Party 2015, National Election Campaign Billboard in Copenhagen   32

1.3 Poster for the "Try on hijab" stand during a university's Islamic Awareness Week, Montreal   33

1.4 Public iftar dinner during Ramadan at Copenhagen Town Hall Square, 2015, Copenhagen   34

4.1 A screenshot of an interactive "socioeconomic" map over Copenhagen with a filter to show the percentage of residents of "non-Western heritage."   78

4.2 The yellow wall of the famous Assistentens Cemetery, where historical figures such as Søren Kierkegaard and HC Andersen are buried   80

4.3 Picture of the inside of *Kaffehuset*   83

4.4 Advert from the Royal Theatre hanging on *Kongens Nytorv*   85

4.5 Hotel D'Angleterre, Copenhagen   86

4.6 Inside the NGO office where Dania volunteers   88

4.7 Blågård Square (*Blågårdsplads*), Nørrebro   89

4.8 Grocery store in Blågårds Square, Nørrebro   91

4.9 Store window on Elmegade, Nørrebro   92

4.10 Large mural in *Kaffehuset*, Nørrebro   93

4.11 Quant antique furniture in *Kaffehuset*, Nørrebro   94

4.12 Inside *Assistentens* Cemetery, Nørrebro   95

4.13 Inside Hamad Bin Khalifa Mosque, Nørrebro   97

4.14 Inside the office building where Khalid works in Hellerup, Copenhagen   98

5.1 Community allotment where Sidra's parents had a plot when they first settled in Montreal   109

5.2	The door to Sidra's first apartment where she and her sister used to practise Bengali writing, Montreal	110
5.3	Sidra's childhood park, Montreal	111
5.4	Inside Sidra's family store, Montreal	112
5.5	Sidra's local mosque, Montreal	113
5.6	Sidra's current home, Montreal	115
5.7	Balcony observed on Amy's walk, where she speaks about looking up when having an artistic bloc, Côte-des-Neiges, Montreal	116
5.8	Saint Joseph's oratory observed during Amy's walk, Côte-des-Neiges, Montreal	118
5.9	Intersection connecting Amy to her different city spaces, Côte-des-Neiges, Montreal	120
5.10	Display table in the bookshop Amy enjoys visiting, Côte-des-Neiges, Montreal	121
5.11	The park where Amy goes to relax and disconnect in the summertime, Côte-des-Neiges, Montreal	122
5.12	Inside the café Amy took me to in Côte-des-Neiges, Montreal	123
5.13	The townhouse where Adam first lived when his family migrated to Canada. West Island, Montreal	124
5.14	The fence where Adam played with the neighbourhood kids, West Island, Montreal	126
5.15	Bus Station at the local mall. This is where Yaqub would take the bus to school and come to hang out at the mall. West Island, Montreal	128
5.16	Yaqub's childhood home where he lived most of his child- and youthhood. West Island, Montreal	129
5.17	Dents in the carports, which are from Yaqub when he used to play hockey. West Island, Montreal	130
5.18	The local Falafel restaurant where Yaqub would go to eat after religious study circles (halaqah)	131
5.19	The local mosque where Yaqub used to come as a child. West Island, Montreal	132
6.1	The Saint Lawrence River at Old Pointe Claire Village, West Island, Montreal	145

Acknowledgements

I want to start by thanking all the participants who allowed me to bear witness to their incredibly vibrant lives, experiences, and movements. If it had not been for their kindness and openness, this book would not have been possible. I am indebted to them all.

I would also like to thank the mosques, organisations, study circles, and Muslim Student Associations that allowed me to participate in their events and advertise my project to their members.

Vered Amit has been an important mentor in the early stages of this research project. Her guidance during my PhD has helped make me a better researcher and scholar. I am sincerely grateful for her support.

I am grateful to *The Sociological Review* for granting me a fellowship to write this research. Without it, this book would not have been written. Thanks to Emma Jackson for providing valuable feedback throughout the early writing stages of this book. Thanks to Lisa Dikomitis, Derek McGhee, and Michaela Benson for their support during my fellowship.

Special thanks to Lamies Nassri, whose constructive feedback to earlier drafts of the book was so helpful. And thanks to Sadia Habib, Khadija Elshayyal, and Reva Jaffe-Walter for reading and providing helpful comments to parts of the book.

Finally, I am indebted to my family for all their love and support. Especially my husband, Tarek Younis, who has patiently read through all the drafts of this book. He has provided invaluable support and inspiration in its completion. His patience and insights have been essential for my dedication to this project.

My children, Aya, Yaqeen, and Ameen, have brought joy to my life. They have been a needed distraction and relief when writing became too overwhelming. A special thanks to my parents, Fatima Almas and Riad Hassani, for always supporting and believing in me. As always, I am grateful to God for the opportunities I was provided and the people who have helped me along the way.

Introduction

Muslims in Colour-Blind Societies

Over the years, Muslims have become a more visible presence within Denmark and Quebec. Their visibility is a consequence of global and local transformations based on the West's global exploitation routes as well as crises, including the post-World War II (WWII) labour migration to Europe, the 1980s' Iranian revolution, postcolonial instabilities, and more recently 9/11 and the War on Terror. It is in the aftermath of this last globalised political crisis—the War on Terror—in which the young Muslims I met during my fieldwork in Copenhagen and Montreal came of age. They grew up in progressive liberal societies that on the surface offered them tremendous opportunities in social and economic mobility and success. The one caveat, however, is that their Muslimness—or perceived Muslimness—is racialised as the "dangerous Other" by the state, and thus needs to be made either invisible or digestible. In tackling the question of Muslim experiences in colour-blind societies, it is necessary to unpack how the racialisation of the Muslim Other is relevant. This is particularly important in Denmark and Quebec where the word "race"—let alone an understanding of racialisation—is non-existent in political, public, and even most academic domains. While there is an explicit erasure of race through a colour-blind rhetoric in these societies, its consequences are omnipresent. This forces us to consider how Muslims in these societies are still racialised, though their racialisation remains implicit. In this sense, it becomes necessary to interrogate how we can understand Muslims—a community of different ethnicities, appearances, and religiosities—as a racialised Other (Garner & Selod, 2015; Sayyid & Vakil, 2010).

This book emphasises the agency of young Muslims within societies which racialise them. It centres "Muslim" within the interplay between self-identification and categorisation, whereby young Muslims are racialised according to ethnonationalist politics and social conflict. Denmark and Quebec are significant sites in this regard. Both contexts have seen an increasing thrust of nationalist politics which position their Muslim citizens as the quintessential Other. In this sense, the book interrogates "the Muslim Question" (Norton, 2013) from the perspective of young Muslims. It investigates how these youth experience, navigate, and contest society's expectations of them in social interactions, public spaces, and in political/media discourses. By focusing on the experiences of racialisation among young Muslims coming

DOI: 10.4324/9781003294696-1

2 Introduction

of age post-9/11, the book centres these youths' pathways and narratives through social spaces.

Situating this book within wider scholarship on racialisation opens up the conversation of the Muslim experience within Denmark and Quebec to a much longer academic trajectory of critical race theory as well as post-colonial scholarship that unpacks these experiences vis-à-vis the racial and imperial hierarchies of these respective nations. In other words, instead of focusing on the Muslim experience as a *Muslim* experience, these experiences are unravelled in connection to wider national(ist) paradigms of the Other. Although both Danish and Quebec political discourses rarely reference their discrepant imperialist histories—the former colonising abroad while the latter existing on colonised territory—the structures of imperialism are the building blocks of their national imaginary. While Denmark perceives itself as the benevolent slave owners in West Indies and civilising colonisers in Greenland (Odumosu, 2019; Olwig, 2003; Thisted, 2018), Quebec imagines its history as French settlers oppressed by English colonisers, erasing their role in the oppression and destruction of indigenous communities and Quebec's role in the transatlantic slave trade (Austin, 2010; Cooper, 2007).

Frames of Colour Blindness

In this introductory chapter, I introduce Denmark and Quebec as colour-blind societies. I do not mean this in actual social, economic, and cultural effects, but rather as a liberal ideology. This ideology allows the racialisation of Muslims and other people of colour, while maintaining an image of egalitarianism and equal opportunities (Hassani, 2023a). To make this argument, it is useful to briefly synthesise the theoretical framework of colour blindness as popularised by Eduardo Bonilla-Silva (2006). In his book *Racism Without Racists* (2006), Bonilla-Silva demonstrates how a colour-blind ideology reproduces racialised social systems. Colour blindness as a powerful mechanism to uphold racialised hierarchies is comprised of four frames, which he defines as "*set paths for interpreting information*" (italics in original, Bonilla-Silva, 2006, p. 26).

The first frame, *abstract liberalism*, individualises racial inequalities. It places the onus on non-white people to extract the benefits of "equal opportunities" and egalitarian policies. Refusing to acknowledge the structural inequalities racialised Others experience, this sort of colour-blind liberalism becomes a way of invisibilising structural racism. The second frame, *naturalisation*, is a way of explaining white segregation (e.g. in housing areas, schools, etc.) as natural occurrences and personal preferences. The third frame, and perhaps the most important for this book, is the idea of *cultural racism*. Cultural racism is a way of racialising non-white people based on signifiers related to their culture or religion. For instance, the idea that Muslim men are inherently violent and oppressive, and Muslim women in turn are subjugated and oppressed are well-known stereotypes ascribed to

Introduction 3

the Muslim community (Razack, 2004). In such a colour-blind framing, rather than focusing on phenotypical signifiers, racism is made invisible by emphasising cultural values as essential, problematic, and incompatible with liberal values. Finally, the last frame of a colour-blind ideology is a *minimisation of racism,* suggesting it is no longer relevant and only expressed by a few individual outliers in society. While not directly referring to Bonilla-Silva, David T. Goldberg's argument in his essay *Racial Europeanization* (Goldberg, 2006) demonstrates this frame by focusing on Europe's racial denial. He argues how European racial denial arose post-WWII. But the erasure of race was never quite accomplished. Rather, racism became individualised and relegated to a few bad apples, while the structural implications of a racial social system were silenced. To paraphrase Goldberg's point to relate to Bonilla-Silva's colour-blind framework: racialisation is made invisible through colour-blind discourse, yet its implications and effects persist.

Focusing on securitisation policies in the UK as part of the War on Terror, Tarek Younis and Sushrut Jadhav (2020) expand on this point of colour blindness by demonstrating how race, while acknowledged superficially in UK counter-terrorism policies, is often erased or denied through a colour-blind veneer. Alana Lentin (2008) argues how race has been replaced with other signifiers such as "culture" and "ethnicity" in Europe. The repercussions of such concepts are, however, still focused on distinguishing real (white) Europeans from non-Europeans. It racialises people of colour without admitting the racial logics underlying such distinctions. As Sivamohan Valluvan (2019, p. 77) puts it, ethnicity is collapsed with race in this regard, where ethnicity and culture are something possessed by racialised Others, while white Europeans occupy a non-ethnic, non-cultural position of neutrality. Following Goldberg's and Lentin's arguments, Fatima El Tayeb (2011) argues that European "racial" understanding has always been a social construct. Thus, the prolific use of "ethnic" is understood as an objective emphasis on regional differences compared to the problematic use of "race." She explains that the use of "ethnicity" indeed produces hierarchised structures that use and produce "ethnic" difference. "Ethnic" is then a site of foreignness that validates European whiteness as authentically European in popular imagination. El Tayeb contends that framing Europe as free of racism is essential to European self-image. Thus, any reference to "race" within a European context challenges the dominant narrative of a colour-blind continent. This colour-blind self-image erases Europe's legacy of racism, resulting in limited explorations of the history and contemporary presence of "race" and racism.

Liberalism, Racism, and Racialised Social System

The dominant narratives in Denmark and Quebec emphasise their progressive, liberal, and welfare ideals—political models for the world to admire. Nevertheless, these nations neglect their colonial histories and the racial

4   *Introduction*

inequalities that persist today. By focusing on Muslim youth coming of age in post-9/11 in Denmark and Quebec, this book challenges the perception that these nations are post-racial egalitarian utopias. It provides a critical and complex analysis of how these two nations are social systems in which a racial hierarchy is infused within both the social and spatial structures. Eduardo Bonilla-Silva's conceptualisation of racialised social systems is useful to think with in this regard, as an expression of how economic, political, social, and ideological structures depend on a racialisation of people (Bonilla-Silva, 1997, p. 469). It is important to take the time in this introduction to conceptualise the very specific forms of what a racialised social system looks like in Denmark and Quebec as it differs from the US context Bonilla-Silva refers to.

Throughout this book, I emphasise the middle-class positioning of the young people I met. This is an alternative approach to neo-Marxist readings of racism, which have tended to give primacy to class inequalities, where class power dynamics are viewed as the root causes of racism (Bonilla-Silva, 2001). By emphasising middle-classness and socioeconomic mobility among young Muslims, I don't seek to discredit the importance of class in discussing Islamophobia and racialisation of Muslims, but rather to complexify the debate. The youth I met often took pride in their position within a growing Muslim middle class. However, despite their class positioning, they could not escape the racialised social structures which they inhabit. In other words, by focusing on middle-classness, I want to challenge the idea that racism, as a way of sustaining inequality within a racialised social system, is merely a limitation for class mobility. Anti-racist/anti-Islamophobic opposition takes on a different shape in these societies when one is part of a middle class. It often becomes a balancing act between being "good"—as in a successful, productive citizen—on the one hand, and resisting the limitations of racialising/Islamophobic legislation and popular debates on the other.

In Quebec, Bill 21 which prohibits public employees from wearing hijab does not care if a woman who wears hijab is a good teacher or physician. Her Muslimness takes primacy, making her education or qualifications irrelevant. While Quebec has introduced Bill 21 with the idea that it will ensure equality between men and women, this very notion demonstrates just how countries can perpetuate racialised subordination based on progressive liberal ideals. These ideals approach gender equality in Eurocentric terms—ironically, by deliberately discriminating against Muslim women in their quest to liberate them. Aurelien Mondon and Aaron Winter (2020) provide a useful framing to understand liberalism as hegemonic rather than equal or just. It is about who has the power over the dominant narrative:

> While the rights that liberalism is argued to have bestowed upon us are unevenly and unequally distributed, they offer us a degree of protection others do not have, and thus come to be accepted by the majority of individual interests and votes, which are seen as the basis of our

democracy. If some should suffer along the way for us to retain these rights, then it is simply argued that democracy has spoken, and that our generosity must have its limits.

(Mondon & Winter, 2020)

The political national(ist) narratives within Denmark and Quebec follow this logic. They are examples of how progressive liberal nationalism can promote a liberal version of racism/Islamophobia against Muslim citizens as a way to uphold power dynamics. In other words, as Gilroy established several decades ago, nationalism and racism are interconnected concepts (Gilroy, 2013). One feeds off the other in a racialised social system. And yet in the two contexts in which this ethnography takes place, nationalism is hailed as the protection of liberal values, while racism is tabooed as non-existent beyond individual prejudice.

Both Quebec and Denmark politically struggle with a perceived lost cultural homogeneity. This "cultural anxiety" (Grillo, 2003) has produced challenging—if not structurally unequal—social circumstances for racialised populations in general and Muslims in particular (Mahrouse, 2010; Bakali, 2015; Benhadjoudja, 2017; Bilge, 2013; Rytter & Pedersen, 2014; Wren, 2001). Nevertheless, both countries have a political and social system that perceives itself as colour-blind. Race is not and has never been a problem (Austin, 2010; Odumoso, 2019). This means that racialising discourse on the Muslim Other becomes hegemonic, yet remains invisible. It is a way to promote culturalist explanations of "essential foreignness" that need "integrating" into progressive liberal values (Omi & Winant, 2014). Similar to both contexts is the erasure of race—not in actual effect, but merely in discourse. One cannot talk of racism—whether structural or individual—although it permeates through society at the political, economic, and social levels.

Racism in this sense is just one way of understanding the racialised components within the social structures of society. The existence of racism, as a phenomenon imbued within social structures, is often characterised as an exceptionally American or British phenomenon arising from their historical foundations in colonialism, the transatlantic slave trade, and in the US South with Jim Crow laws. Instead, the national political debates on racism—and its structural underpinnings—are disregarded for an ideological definition of racism that in Denmark often roots itself in German Nazism (WWII) and in Quebec, with Anglophone imperialism of French Canadians. The former neglects the history of Danish imperialism (Jensen, 2018), and the latter neglects French colonisation of indigenous lands (Austin, 2010). The prevalence of this understanding of racism has meant that there is limited research on racism as a structural phenomenon within these contexts. Instead, if racism is studied at all, it is often perceived as an individual offence within institutions, media, etc., with limited work being done to understand the structural underpinnings of racism.

6   *Introduction*

By focusing on overt and intentional racism, we are left with plenty of surveys and studies asking if you would want Muslims to be kicked out of the country (Andersen & Reiermann, 2019), but little exploration as to the racist underpinnings of even asking such a question. By understanding racism as a by-product of racialisation within a racialised social system, the emphasis is on how it rationalises the structures of racialised inequalities as well as racist encounters in everyday life (Bonilla-Silva, 1997, p. 474). In the Danish and Quebecois contexts, the racialisation of the Muslim Other becomes commonsensical rather than problematic. Muslims are here understood as non-Western, misogynistic, and backwards, and they are not loyal citizens of "our nation." What is important to draw from this is how the racialisation of Others—even in nations such as Denmark and Quebec, where the population is over 90–95% white—becomes fundamental to upholding power dynamics within society.

The Civilised Nation and the "Threatening" Other

In her book on Dutch racism—*White Innocence*—Gloria Wekker (2016) introduces us to a conceptual framework to understand how racism plays out in societies that have neither dealt with their colonial past nor the entrenched racialised structures that have resulted from this past. The Netherlands is an interesting example to compare to both Denmark and Quebec. The Netherlands perceives itself as a benevolent small and just welfare society. With this self-perception, the very notion of racialisation and racism as an integral part of the social structures beyond an individualised expression cannot be entertained. In all three societies, the concept of race is almost non-existent. Instead, the idea of ethnicity and other cultural signifiers are emphasised to highlight foreignness and non-belonging in the guise of "inclusion" through integration into white hegemonic Danish values (Rytter, 2019). Similarly, in Quebec, interculturalism is emphasised, which prioritises French cultural and linguistic heritage (Sharify-Funk, 2010).

Wekker (2016) unpacks how race and racialisation within the dominant discourses—in national politics, media, and popular entertainment—goes unchecked because of the national(ist) image of the country's progressive liberalism. While Wekker traces the Dutch history of racism to its colonial past, specifically focusing on anti-Black racism, Nadia Fadil (2010) connects this idea of the benevolent welfare state to the notion of Islamophobia. Focusing on the Flanders-speaking region in Belgium, Fadil highlights how in Flanders discourse there is a racialised differentiation between *autochton* (native Dutch) and *allochton* (racialised to non-Western people of colour). In Denmark, it is the difference between Danish and non-Western immigrants and descendants (an official category to differentiate non-white people from white "Westeners," which includes the US, Canada, Australia, and New Zealand). For more than 20 years, non-Westerners have been racialised

Introduction 7

as Muslim in Denmark (Yilmaz, 2016). In Quebec, it is the differentiation between *Quebecois des souche* or *Quebecois pur laine*[1] (Austin, 2010) and its "cultural communities," i.e. racialised Others, who are culturally, religiously, and linguistically differentiated from "real French Quebecers" rooted in the land.

Comparatively in these cases is a national image of progressive liberal values, which are inadvertently threatened by the Muslim's illiberalness. Fadil explains this point, describing how Muslims' lives "which fall outside the liberal spectrum, are seen as 'barbaric', incapable of similar liberal values, and even potentially 'threatening' to one's own liberal lifestyle" (2010, p. 249). This dichotomy between the civilised Nation and the threatening Other is not a new phenomenon but has fuelled much of nationalist rhetoric in the guise of national exceptionalism. While none of the popular imageries of the nation within these countries would admit a racist past, not to mention a racist present, there is an image of national(ist) exceptionalism based on its progressive welfare. If we understand nationalism as a boundary-making process in which people perceived as Others are excluded, the argument introduced by Gilroy over three decades ago becomes essential to understand how nationalism within these colour-blind progressive liberal societies is deeply interconnected with racism (Gilroy, 2013).

Understanding Islamophobia

This book takes a phenomenological approach by focusing on young Muslims' lived experiences and being-in-the-world (Jackson, 1996). Nevertheless, their experiences cannot be disconnected from the structural realities which privilege whiteness and its proximities (Gullestad, 2002). Thus, a phenomenological approach must be combined with a critical framework that gives attention to wider structural phenomena of racism and nationalism (Gilroy, 2013b). In other words, the focus is not merely on how young Muslims experience interpersonal racism or Islamophobia from white individuals. Rather, the focus is also on the racialised social system that influences most areas of Muslims' and other racialised peoples' lives. It is the implicit awareness of this social system that enables the young Muslims I met to navigate racist encounters in everyday interactions and spatial mobilities.

There have been decades of critical race scholarship which has demonstrated how the US operates as a racialised social system (Anderson, 2022; Bonilla-Silva, 2001; Omi & Winant, 2014). It is, however, more controversial in both Denmark and Quebec to suggest these societies encompass a racialised hierarchy. The fact remains, however, that as soon as there is a public perception of who "real" Danes/Quebeckers are, there is also a racialisation of the Other, which will intrinsically affect the everyday lives and

---

1 Quebeckers rooted in the land (*des souches*) or of "clean wool" (*pure laine*).

8 *Introduction*

livelihoods of these people. In this sense, we need to unpack what it means for Muslims—in all their heterogeneity—to be racialised as Other within a racialised social system. According to Garner and Selod (2015), racialisation is a tool for the rulers to implement on the ruled:

> [i]t draws a line around all the members of the group; instigates 'group-ness', and ascribes characteristics, sometimes because of work, some-times because of ideas of where the group comes from, what it believes in, or how it organizes itself socially and culturally.
>
> (2015, p. 15)

The point is that racialisation is not the same as self-ascription, i.e. Muslims feeling a sense of community based on similar religious beliefs. Rather, racialisation operates through power structures that perpetuate the racial-ised systems (e.g. governments, mainstream media, entertainment indus-try). These racialised representations "transform the clearly culturally and phenotypically dissimilar individuals [...] into a homogenous bloc: this is the basis of the racialization of Muslims (the process), and of Islamophobia (the snapshot of outcomes of this process)" (Garner & Selod, 2015, p. 15). Islamophobia— as with racism in general—is thus a by-product of a racial-ised social system (Sayyid, 2010). Tarek Younis expands on this by defining Islamophobia as a way to manage ideal Muslim subjectivity (Younis, 2023). The management of Muslim subjectivity is a useful way to conceptualise Islamophobia, as it allows us to understand how the young Muslims in this book navigate the boundaries of acceptability vis-à-vis their Muslimness in terms of positioning themselves as middle-class *Danish/Quebecois(e)* Muslims.

In both the Danish and Quebec contexts, critical scholars have demon-strated how the racialisation of Muslims has developed. In the Danish case, Ferruh Yilmaz (2016) provides a revealing analysis of how immigrant "guest workers" became Muslim in public and political consciousness. In the Quebec case, Sirma Bilge (2013) as well as Leila Benhadjoudja (Benhadjoudja, 2017) depict the racialised logics behind who receives a public platform to discuss ideas of liberalism and secularism. In contrast, there are those who are left with little avenue to resist these ideas but must adhere to the legislation that limits their agency—often racialised Muslims, particularly women wearing the hijab and niqab.

With this understanding of the racialisation of Muslims as a process to Otherise them, our attention is drawn to the physical markers through dress, phenotypical signifiers, and also their practices of Muslimness, such as daily prayers, fasting, and halal food. In this sense, it is not only the exter-nal signs of Muslimness that are racialised, but the very practice of Islam that is Othered. The white convert Muslims I spoke to were therefore not shielded from this racialisation. For instance, one white young woman

Introduction 9

in Montreal, Amy,[2] explained how as soon as people found out she was Muslim, they would assume she was of Arab origin. Likewise, a young man from Montreal, Adam, who was of Iranian descent but raised Christian, was often assumed to be Muslim even before his conversion based on both his phenotypical appearance and his political opinions (e.g. being critical of American imperialism).

The racialisation of Muslims and structural expressions of Islamophobia are ways for political powers to curb and limit Muslim agency (Sayyid, 2010) and manage Muslim subjectivity (Younis, 2023). This tells us something about the social structures and how racialised power dynamics are upheld from the top, trickling down to real-life consequences in social interactions as well as life chances (e.g. educational limitations, employment opportunities, housing inequalities). They create a powerful infrastructure of subordination through which Muslims in these societies must navigate (Massoumi et al., 2017, pp. 13–14). I use the concept of Islamophobia throughout this book, not merely as religious discrimination, but to emphasise how structures of power racialise Muslims as a quintessential Other—a diametrical opposite to the imagined homogenous (white) Us. This type of structural Islamophobia is promoted through political discourse and mainstreaming of anti-Muslim racism (Hafiz, 2022).

Agency as Capacity to Act

Agency is a helpful concept to think with throughout the ethnographic narratives presented in this book. To define agency, it is important to briefly sketch out its importance in critical and feminist scholarship. It has often been thought of as an empowering concept of resistance to mobilise against structures of oppression (Mahmood, 2011). However, this is not always what is happening among the middle-class Muslims I met in Montreal and Copenhagen. They were not necessarily actively resisting political powers, but often manoeuvring around and through them to establish their social position while also insisting on their right to religious expression. To be able to understand these manoeuvrings, it is helpful to look at Saba Mahmood's conceptualisation of agency as she observed it among Muslim women's involvement in the Islamic revival in Egypt. She builds on the scholarship of Lila Abu-Lughod (1990), who provides a critical reflection of some of her earlier work on resistance practices among Bedouin women in Egypt. Abu-Lughod suggests that feminist scholarship has often been too focused

---

2 All names of participants are pseudonyms, and any identifying details have been removed to protect their confidentiality. All interviews in Montreal were conducted in English. Most interviews in Denmark were conducted in Danish and subsequently translated by me, except for one interview that was conducted in English and therefore did not need translation.

10   *Introduction*

on understanding resistance as an approach to challenge power. However, she critiques, when we attempt to read resistance as a failure of systems of oppression, we fail to appreciate resistance as a "diagnostic of power" (Abu-Lughod, 1990, p. 42). In other words, we must move beyond the binary of resistance/subordination to understand how specific forms of resistance must be located within fields of power.

Building on Abu-Lughod's reflections on resistance, Mahmood takes the discussion one step further by questioning whether acts of resistance can ever be universalised. Rather, she argues, these acts should always be read within the local ethical and political conditions where they are attributed certain meanings (Mahmood, 2011, p. 9). Moving away from an emphasis on resistance, Mahmood argues for a concept of agency that is open to "semantic and institutional networks that define and make possible particular ways of relating to people, things and oneself" (Asad in Mahmood, 2011, p. 34). Mahmood summarises how agency sometimes does in fact mean resistance against power, but as a concept needs to be unpacked through the nexus of ethics and politics (Mahmood, 2011, p. 34). She thus defines agency as a *capacity for action* enabled by a particular context. Adopting Mahmood's conceptualisation of agency as a capacity for action rather than explicit resistance to circumvent structures of power opens up the concept to alternative perspectives beyond resistance. The young people I met in both Denmark and Quebec did not necessarily actively mobilise against Islamophobic policies and everyday racist experiences. Rather, they navigate through such experiences by rooting themselves within the urban context through spatial narratives. In other words, their capacity to act as middle-class Muslims meant that they had an agency that allowed them to secure their middle-class positions and challenge racist and Islamophobic rhetoric experienced in everyday interactions through such class positioning. Mahmood's opening of the concept of agency can thus be complexified even further through an intersectional lens (Crenshaw, 1990). It is not only the broader political context that allows particular forms of agency, but signifiers of class, racialisation, and gender allow different capacities for action. In this way, young Muslims' ability to evade racist discourses was contingent on their ability to position themselves through gendered/racialised/classed signifiers within a particular narrative of the respectable Muslim in contrast to the inferiorisation of Muslims dominant in political discourse.

The Muslim Subject

Throughout this book, it is important to appreciate how young Muslims contest and navigate social and political structures. Islamophobia—as a racism towards Muslimness or perceived Muslimness—is becoming increasingly entrenched within the political and populistic landscape in both Denmark and Quebec (Benhadjoudja, 2017; Rytter & Pedersen, 2014). By approaching "Muslim" not only as a religious self-ascription, but also as a racialised categorisation, I want to draw attention towards a more nuanced and complex understanding of what it means to be identified as Muslim in these two cities. I am interested in how young Muslims navigate and negotiate racialisation of their Muslimness, whether because of phenotypical signifiers, their hijab, beards, or some other signifiers that society around them imagines to be particularly Muslim. In this sense, their Muslimness is politicised, seen as a quintessential Other (cf. Norton, 2013; Sayyid, 2010). Their "foreignness"—often exoticised or vilified—is always omnipresent.

The chapters that follow explore how young middle-class Muslims carve out their positions within such societies. The young people I met were adamant about *being* a part of and being *seen* as part of these cities and nations. They resisted—sometimes explicitly, but often implicitly—attempts to undermine their belonging. This is similar to what Sadia Habib found in her study of young British Muslims, whose sense of belonging is often impacted by their social positioning and opportunities to construct counter-narratives of Britishness (Habib, 2017).

One of the earliest and most influential thinkers in American sociology, WEB Du Bois (2008 [1903]), provides a helpful reference to understand how racialised people internalise their racialisation through double consciousness. They "learn to read themselves through the eyes and mindsets of the majority population and regulate their behaviour accordingly in specific contexts" (Garner & Selod, 2015, p. 17). The idea of double consciousness is woven into many of the narratives presented throughout the chapters of this book. While it is expressed differently in Copenhagen and Montreal, all the youth I engaged with had to deal with ways of being racialised as Muslims and acted accordingly. They negotiated their groupness (i.e. the construction of the Muslim community, cf. Brubaker, 2004), their self-representation as a model minority, and their position within social spaces often as a *response* to their racialisation.

Otherisation as a form of subordination, in this sense, does not curb all capacity for action. Nevertheless, the capacity to resist and contest the power dynamics is limited to hegemonic narratives. For example, most of the young Muslims I met did not necessarily resist the nationalist framing of Danish/ Quebecois exceptionalism, but rather rephrased the framing to emphasise their rootedness within these "exceptional" societies (see also Koefoed, 2015). Likewise, they were not necessarily invested in challenging the class hierarchies which placed Muslims on the lower end of this pendulum. Rather, they invested their energy in demonstrating their rightful position as contributing middle-class citizens. They thereby challenged the idea of Muslim inferiority based on their class mobility. This attention to class position was particularly pronounced in the Danish context, where Muslims are racialised as economically marginalised. In Quebec, on the other hand, the question of class is more complex and closely related to linguistic differences. French-speaking Muslims often originating from French post-colonies tend to be more recent migrants and therefore less economically secure. While English-speaking or

12   *Introduction*

bilingual Muslims are often already placed within more privileged positions given their migration history often as professionals. Going back to my point of agency then, the young people I met had a capacity to challenge, rephrase, and reframe the presumptions of their political subordination, but they were not necessarily able to dismantle, disempower, or circumvent these structures of power.

Muslims' religious identification in both field sites was often conflated with migrant identification. Sometimes this was a form of self-identification, but more often than not by the world around them: Muslim = foreign/non-Western. This conflation is a symptom of their positioning as the quintessential Other within nationalist rhetoric. Such a narrative of Muslim-racialisation tells us little about Muslims' lives, experiences, and their relationship to the social spaces they inhabit and their positioning within these. We risk overlooking how young Muslims find creative and implicit ways to contest the Danish and Quebec states' attempts to control and influence the social and spatial contexts in which they live in.

My focus on Muslim experiences is not a way to explore a distinct religious minority and their "cultural/religious practises." Rather, the book focuses on the experiences of racialisation, drawing our attention to the power dynamics at play to uphold the structures of dominance. Any attention to this from the perspective of Muslims' experiences inadvertently becomes an attention to the creative ways these youth challenge, negotiate, and navigate through such power dynamics. The book thus unpacks the experiences of racialisation in colour-blind progressive liberal societies, where the academic scholarship surrounding Muslims has too often focused on their "foreignness"; i.e. their religious organisation, integration processes, cultural differences, transnational ties. This has somewhat skewed the academic conversations, possibly even helped reproduce the political reification of Muslims as Other in Denmark and Quebec. The result is little attention given to structural power dynamics through which Muslim citizens are surveilled and managed, and their social lives scrutinised and intervened.

Navigation as a Mobility Approach

The concept of mobility in both social and spatial terms is an important conceptual frame for this book. In his book, *Mobilities* , John Urry argues for an approach to understanding mobility as a paradigm, encompassing an understanding of "how all social entities, from single households to large scale corporations, presuppose many different forms of actual and potential movement" (Urry, 2007, p. 6). Urry expands the definition of mobility to include a more multi-stranded concept of understanding, which includes physical but also social mobility. Connecting Urry's mobilities approach to the broader theoretical argument I am making in this chapter, a mobilities approach allows for an emphasis on the fluidity of the assemblages in both conceptual and spatial terms.

Introduction 13

In spatial terms, an approach that emphasises movement through space helps demonstrate the interconnection between spaces to broader social and political processes. This is particularly relevant here, since the young Muslims presented in the third part of the book utilised the spatial tours to demonstrate both their spatial and social mobility. Their movements within city spaces demonstrated their ability to navigate the social structures, i.e. choosing to go to one neighbourhood for its positive social connotations while dismissing a nearby neighbourhood for its stigmatised associations. Their spatial mobility was also a representation of time, i.e. depicting past experiences and connections to localities or describing future aspirations and expectations through their movements. Finally, these young people represented their own social mobility through their spatial narratives, i.e. from growing up in an inner-city neighbourhood to becoming successful university students and middle-class professionals.

The mobility paradigm promoted by Urry draws attention to the wide range of movements people make in the course of their lives. Indeed, there is an increasing awareness of how "moving people construct and reconstruct places, social relations and social contexts in the course of and through their ongoing experiences of movement" (Amit & Olwig, 2011). In this sense, it is about people's capacities, social context, and ability to improvise when they move. Caroline Knowles argues that understanding movements enables us to understand how we are formed by the places we go to and the way we get there—it is thus a way to understand subjectivities (Knowles, 2011, p. 139). This requires our understanding of people's movements to be contextualised within a broader understanding of their lives, their aspirations, and their closest social ties. In the context of this book, it also requires our understanding of the political and racialised structures Muslims have to navigate through in their everyday lives, which is the focus of the second part of this book. Within such a context, Muslims' movements through particular spaces can be seen as ways of transforming, contesting, or negotiating their social positioning as racialised Others.

Building on this conceptualisation of mobility, I use what I call spatial narratives to explore how young Muslims use, relate, and navigate through city spaces. I walked (and sometimes drove) with them around city spaces that were meaningful to them. This method proved to be valuable in terms of expanding my understanding of these young people's biographies, subjectivities, and mobility in ways that interviewing and participant observation did not reveal. The spatial tours allowed for an appreciation of young Muslims' rootedness, which was manifested through the ease of their movements, the histories they attached to spatial structures, and the negative and positive associations they attributed to particular city districts. However, it becomes important to situate these young Muslims within the wider national(ist) frames of Muslim Othering. They move through spaces that represent this Othering on a daily basis, yet their lives cannot be reduced to this Othering. Many of the youth I met responded to such conflicts with social actions and

14 *Introduction*

protest; yet this was only one part of a much more complex and less dramatic regime of everyday life.

By concentrating on the uses of space, de Certeau illustrates how imposed structures can become reliable, thereby enabling the individual to develop tactics to manipulate these structures (de Certeau, 2005 [1984], p. xxii). De Certeau describes tactics as "an art of the weak." In other words, tactics are the creative responses of non-powerful actors in moments of conjunctures within an imposed structural terrain of hegemonic power (ibid., p. 37). In the context of my fieldwork, young Muslims demonstrated their tactical abilities through their spatial narratives. These tactics were revealed through the movements and narratives expressed during the walks we went on. For instance, Khadija—a young woman living in social housing in Copenhagen—chose to avoid some parts of Copenhagen, and instead focused on downtown Copenhagen, thus highlighting her ability to socially navigate the social structures that were entrenched in these city spaces. Some spaces represented lower socioeconomic status while other spaces represented affluence. Khadija's choices of the spaces to include in her account demonstrated her acute awareness of her own self-representation through these city structures. This is where her tactical skills became important; they provided her an opportunity to represent her quest for social mobility within social structures over which she had little power. In other words, the concept of everyday tactics allows an appreciation of how young people, such as Khadija, construct creative attempts to manipulate the hidden potentials within societal structures to claim their social position within their city spaces.

The focus is thus on understanding how one is able to manoeuvre within racialised structures. It is through one's creative manoeuvreing that one can develop a certain—if limited—measure of autonomy in spite of the hegemonic structures of society (de Certeau, 2005, p. 176). In the context of spatial tours, de Certeau's perspective on space becomes an important avenue through which to understand young Muslims' attachments to their localities. The city is ingrained in their memories and pathways in the same way they, in turn, influence the city spaces through their presence and practices. In other words, it is through their everyday movements that young Muslims become an integral part of the city's heterogeneous spaces.

Throughout this book, I use the concept of navigation as a way to describe young Muslims' agency within a sociopolitical field that is rapidly changing. Henrik Vigh (Vigh, 2009) offers a useful conceptualisation of navigation as a "motion within motion." In other words, navigation is the way social actors move amidst terrains/social structures that are themselves constantly shifting. Young Muslims' navigation involved different discursive tactics, which they utilised when they experienced overt, covert, or even structural racism. Navigation thus highlights how these youth consciously use their spaces: to insist on their belonging, to resist their exclusion, and to affirm their entitlement to certain (white) professional/social spaces.

Participants and Urban Ethnographic Methods

In the course of a year-long fieldwork divided between Copenhagen and Montreal, I engaged with over 50 young Muslims (18- to 25-year-olds). The ethnographic material that forms the foundation for this book's analysis consists of qualitative interviews, participant observation, and spatial narratives. Throughout the book, I have chosen to include longer case and narrative-based sections of a few interlocutors, rather than attempt to provide an overview of all 50 participants' experiences. Instead, as a qualitative comparative ethnography, this book presents unique stories that share similarities across my participant cohort, yet they also offer nuanced and complex reflections that force us to rethink and question any attempts to represent Muslims as a homogenous monolith.

I lived in Montreal for most of the year's fieldwork and divided my fieldtrip to Copenhagen into two longer visits at the beginning and end of my fieldwork year. The participant observations I did in both sites were often dependent on what was going on in the city at the time in terms of protests, rallies, and public events. However, as I became more acquainted with many of my participants, they would invite me along to weddings, birthday parties, or just join their book club or hang out in the Muslim Student Association office. These all expanded my understanding and appreciation of the social context in which they lived in. The qualitative interviews I conducted were semi-structured and focused on their life experiences, often with an emphasis on their experiences as a "Muslim minority." Finally, the urban tours the Muslim young adults took me on and the spatial narratives they formulated through these walks opened up the narrative potential beyond experiences of racialisation.

Urban Walks as Ethnographic Tools

There was a unique ethnographic potential in allowing the young people to guide me through the spaces they related to. If we see cities as interactions (Simmel, 1997), then we must also consider how these interactions become sites of negotiating social position and meaning making. Being visibly Muslim myself and only a few years older than my interlocutors gave me a unique position within these two cities as well as in relation to the young Muslims I engaged with. We navigated these city spaces together embodying the signs of racialisation that dominate political and media discourse on Muslims. Throughout the walks, the experience of racialisation was seldom made explicit. In fact, in both cities, they often seemed conscious as to when to direct my attention to racialised "white spaces" (Anderson, 2022) and when to demand my attention be directed elsewhere. For instance, how the spaces we walked through said something about who they were, where they grew up, and how these spaces were in fact *theirs* to inhabit, walk through, and ultimately represent as part of "their city."

16   *Introduction*

I asked the young Muslims I met to take me on a tour of their city, leaving the question broad and open to their interpretation. This resulted in rich ethnographic material depicting their unique histories, social positions, and subjectivities. Moving with them while listening to their reasoning and narratives for imbuing certain spaces with particular importance—and undermining other spaces' importance—helped me appreciate these young people's positioning within and connection to their city. Thus, they were able to display their agency through their narrative choices. They chose which spaces, the directions, the stories of the past, images of the present, or imaginaries of the future they wanted to emphasise. The interviews I had conducted with all of them before their spatial tours only demonstrated one side of their lives. The interviews were limited by my own analytical scope, what I thought was important to ask about and what I thought was important to represent. The tours, however, incorporated the young Muslims in the epistemological process of ethnography. They were doing ethnography with me, and they were instilling this ethnography with analytical potential through their narratives and reflections as we walked through their city spaces.

They were all young, between the ages of 18 and 25 years, from Montreal or Copenhagen, who self-identified as Muslims, but were also racialised as Muslims by society around them. Nevertheless, their spatial narratives beyond these similar external factors demonstrate the extensive and important nuances that pose implicit questions about the nature of ethnographic representation. How can we, as ethnographers, represent people who share certain categorical identifications (in this case, being Muslim, young, and urban) without risk reducing the lived complexity to simplistic representation (Brubaker, 2002). Following young Muslims' localised urban pathways—taking into account the temporal and social aspects of their narratives—highlights how a focus on spatial accounts provided these youth with a narrative tool that allowed them to demonstrate more nuances than they could depict in the qualitative interviews. In other words, mobility as a methodological tool has the potential to expand our understanding of our participants' use of space in various ways, allowing access to different aspects of their lives. Moving with people also has the potential to challenge the bias social researchers inevitably bring to our research. Hence, by allowing our participants to take charge of the directions we walk—describing what is important to notice and what meanings they attribute to different spaces—they expand the perspectives of our analytical representations beyond the limitations of a sit-down qualitative interview.

Setting the Fields: Copenhagen and Montreal

There has been an exponential rise in ethnonationalist political discourse in both Denmark and Quebec. Although there is an official divide between religion and state, it is often the appearance of non-Christian religious symbols that seems to be the focal point of political rhetoric. Nevertheless,

Copenhagen and Montreal are often celebrated as culturally diverse, vibrant, charming cities, and they thrive on their increased cultural diversity. As harbour cities, Montreal and Copenhagen have historically been the landing ground for merchants and immigrants alike. Since these two cities are both business and cultural hubs of their region, young people have tended to gravitate to these cities from the surrounding rural areas.

While Copenhagen and Montreal enjoy this centralised position within their region, they are still far smaller in scale compared to global cities such as London, Paris, and New York. Montreal and Copenhagen are on the periphery of these global centres since they are smaller in size, population, and global importance. As such, increased plurality and multiculturalism of the cities are situated differently here than in the global cities. While research on young Muslims has often focused on global cities, we lack an appreciation of young Muslims' experiences in more peripheral cities such as Montreal and Copenhagen. These two cities' approaches to pluralism and diversity can provide important insights into how young Muslims navigate and engage with their local surroundings, which is often very different from young Muslims' experiences in global cities.

Copenhagen and Montreal, as the most socially and culturally diverse cities in their regions, provide an important avenue through which to explore the cities' regional and global positioning. Hannerz (1996) suggests focusing on a city's position at a global level. He differentiates between the cultural production processes in peripheral cities, which are cities that do not have a strong place on a global scale, and centre cities, such as London, New York, and Paris, which are positioned as global centres (Hannerz, 1996, p. 77). As field sites, Copenhagen and Montreal provided rich opportunities to explore how young Muslims contribute to their city's positioning. Although most of the youth I engaged with were not migrants themselves but descendants of migrants, their visibility and movements through different city spaces became a reciprocal cycle where their self-representations as socially and spatially mobile urbanites in turn enhanced the city's image as culturally diverse. In other words, these young Muslims moved through the cities in efforts to represent their social mobility, while these very movements in turn enabled the cities to represent themselves as global cities through their culturally diverse populations.

The Structure of the Book

The book is organised into six main chapters preceded by an introduction and followed by a conclusion. The chapters are divided into two main parts: (1) Muslim racialisation and its affects and (2) Muslim pathways and spatial narratives. Chapters 1–3 form the first part of the book and emphasise how the racialisation of Muslims plays out socially in gendered and class-based ways, and thus how processes of racialisation affect young Muslims differently. The second part of the book comprises Chapters 4–6 and demonstrates

18 *Introduction*

how racialisation is spatialised in social and temporal ways and how young Muslims relate and root themselves within their urban spaces.

Chapter 1 presents a theoretical framework of assemblages to unpack racialisation processes in colour-blind societies. The chapter draws on comparative ethnographic material from Copenhagen and Montreal to understand the processes of racialisation in these societies. It thus interrogates the ways Muslims in these two societies negotiate, challenge, and contest the assemblages of their racialisation social and spatial interactions.

Based on ethnography from Copenhagen, Chapter 2 looks at how my Danish participants represent their middle-class positioning and social mobility in a political context, where Muslims' cultural and social belonging is often questioned. The narratives presented in the chapter emphasise the complexities of middle-class social positioning in a political context that often seeks to racialise Muslims as socioeconomically inferior. The ethnographic examples I present in this chapter indicate that these youth—while insisting on their right to religious expression—traverse a racialised terrain to achieve upward social mobility through middle-class respectability.

Chapter 3 discusses the political controversy surrounding the hijab during the *Charter of Values* debate and the Quebec government's attempt to ban it from public spaces. Based on these women's mobilisation against the Charter, the chapter interrogates the process of representing and creating the group. It critiques social groups as a taken-for-granted concept rather than viewing them as something to analyse. On the contrary, the concept of groupness focuses on the process of making the group. I discuss this process of groupness by focusing on how Montreal Muslim women experience being racialised in general society and how they have responded to and mobilised against the Charter debate.

The first chapter in Part II, Chapter 4, turns the focus back to Copenhagen to understand how movement through city spaces can become avenues to challenge cartographies of racialisation. The chapter demonstrates how young Muslims move seamlessly through racialised spaces, invading "white spaces," to construct and represent social mobility and challenge the racialisation of socioeconomic inferiority. The spatial narratives explored in this chapter demonstrate different experiences of social and spatial mobility, and yet similar notions of space as representative of current and prospective social positions.

Chapter 5 interrogates processes of settlement and rootedness through the spatial narratives of the young Montrealers I met. These youth weaved a spatial life narrative through the spaces they showed me. In the process, the spaces became autobiographic, enriched by nostalgic meaning and highlighting important life moments. The chapter explores concepts of rootedness as processual and dynamic, demonstrating how young Muslims are embedded in their urban spaces, and thus contribute to the spatialisation of the city by their presence and use of the city.

Introduction 19

In the final chapter of Part II, Chapter 6, I provide a comparative analysis between my participants' spatial narratives in the two cities and discuss the ethnographic benefit of moving with people to understand the nuances of temporality, subjectivity, and movement. I bring together the ethnographic materials presented in the previous two chapters, drawing comparisons between the young adults I met in Copenhagen and Montreal.

The concluding chapter emphasises how a critical approach to understanding racialisation as (1) a social process and (2) a spatial process enables a complex understanding of young Muslims' capacity to act, negotiate, and navigate through their racialisation in colour-blind societies. This approach emphasises the creative ways Muslims deal—both socially and spatially—with hegemonic racialised structures in colour-blind societies. The conclusion highlights how a comparative perspective of young Muslims' urban lives in the Global North contributes to the wider field of urban ethnography. It demonstrates the importance of an urban perspective, providing a nuanced illustration of Muslims' experiences of and responses to racialisation.

Part I

Muslim Racialisation and its Affects

1 Assemblages of Muslim Racialisation

What happens when we start to unpack the idea of a colour-blind society? In such a society, racialised hierarchies are neglected and racism is invisibilised through colour-blind frames. However, rather than make "racism" disappear, it becomes omnipresent. This is done through racialisation processes that produce Others that are presented as diametrically opposite to Us. In this chapter, I present a framework of assemblages to unpack how colour blindness reproduces the racialisation of the Muslim Other.

Race rarely figures as a native term within Denmark and Quebec. It is assumed to be something that other *more* imperial nations have, such as the US or UK. This chapter shifts the focus from the US and UK in the conversation of "race," and instead emphasises societies that rarely acknowledge any racialised hierarchies. Rather, as colour-blind progressive societies, they have established a national image of egalitarianism, meritocracy, and equal opportunities. I want to challenge this perception through the lens of Muslims' positioning within these two societies. Focusing on racialisation *processes* instead of a categorical analysis of "race," I emphasise the dynamic and fluid process of racialising Others, and in the context of this book, particularly Muslims. With racialisation processes, our attention is directed towards social, cultural, material, and phenotypical signifiers instead of "biologic" essentialist notions of "race." Understanding racialisation processes as part of an assemblage enables us to recognise the social and urban spaces Muslims navigate through as part of a whole that is comprised of components that are interrelated and intersubjective. In turn, we shift our focus from "race"/"ethnicity" to an awareness of the often implicit processes of racialisation that ripple through social and spatial contexts.

As will become clear throughout the book, most of the young people I met were either part of a comfortable middle class or had achieved social mobility through higher education. Almost in contrast to this book's introduction as well as this chapter, these young Muslims in both Copenhagen and Montreal would rarely speak of racism, Islamophobia, or experiencing the effects of an increasingly hostile political discourse towards Muslims and other racialised minorities. Instead, their narratives were filled with positive experiences—of supportive school environments, sports clubs, religious communities, and of "ethnic" shops and restaurants that expand borders and communities. Even

DOI: 10.4324/9781003294696-3

24 *Muslim Racialisation and its Affects*

the blatantly racist experiences they endured as they moved through public spaces and everyday social interactions were downplayed as unimportant to their lives in general. It would be easy to use these narratives to confirm that Denmark and Quebec are in fact post-racial societies. However, in this chapter, I contend that these narratives are essential to understanding what is going on within the deeply racialised yet imagined colour-blind societies that are Denmark and Quebec.

I introduce assemblage theory in this chapter to conceptualise how the process of racialisation trickles down from dominant political and media discourses to their material expression in urban spaces and in everyday social life. Racialisation processes thus influence intersubjective experiences and interactions. Such interactions are not always examples of racist encounters, but sometimes depict the double consciousness that Muslims have adopted while growing up during an era of heightened racialisation and structural infringement on Muslims' rights. The chapter then moves on to explore the urban spaces the young Muslims navigate through. Political campaigns often filled public spaces as a constant reminder of the white gaze over the Muslim Other. Nevertheless, Muslims in Copenhagen and Montreal's diverse spaces seemed to find creative ways to challenge, circumvent, and sometimes redefine these spaces by taking over the political attempts to invisibilise and make them non-relevant to the city image. Instead, by invading these public spaces by their mere presence, and other times by their transforming of a space to become a marker of Muslimness or Muslim solidarity, they found ways to challenge the image of the white hegemonic nation.

Racialisation Assemblages: Between Process and Socio-spatial Affect

Thinking of racialisation as a process within a larger social system invites us to think about what components sum up this process. This is where the idea of assemblages becomes useful. As a concept that focuses on the interconnectedness and fluidity of entities, it allows us to explore racialisation processes in political, social, and spatial formulations and their effects on both white and racialised (in this context: Muslim) populations. At the same time, it allows for these formulations to remain fluid according to time and context. Assemblages are useful to think with because although they allow for power dynamics to play a factor, they do not pre-empt them. In other words, racialisation processes involve powerful actors, who can dominate social and spatial imaginaries of the racialised Other, but their affect is part of the analytical process. This approach allows social actors a level of agency, *a capacity to act*. In other words, it allows white actors to either undermine or reproduce these processes, and it allows racialised Muslims to internalise, circumvent, or challenge these processes. As an analytical tool, assemblages thus allow us to scrutinise different entities within the assemblage without instilling them with *a priori* qualifiers.

Assemblages of Muslim Racialisation   25

My approach to assemblages builds on Alexander G. Weheliye's (2014) idea of racialised assemblages as sociopolitical and relational, and Jasbir Puar's (2018) conceptualisation of assemblages as intersectional. With this approach, I introduce a way of contextualising and relationalising the way Muslims in Denmark and Quebec experience, narrate, and sometimes undermine or disregard sociopolitical processes of racialisation. In other words, there is an assemblage between political discourse of racialising Muslims; the racialisation of public spaces; the way these ideas are adopted by the white majority; and finally, the experiences and response of Muslims in these two societies. Both Weheliye and Puar draw on Delueze and Guettari's assemblage theory to conceptualise their approach. However, instead of synthesising the details of Delueze and Guettari's theory, I use the idea of assemblage theory as summarised by Weheliye as well as Puar to think with as a backdrop to understand society in general. What is relevant for this chapter is to appreciate the relationality of all components within society. The idea of viewing society as an assemblage helps us to understand the interconnected processes of racialisation. There is an important link between political discourse on Muslims (and racialised Others in general) and the ripples this discourse creates throughout society both in material terms (images of dangerous Muslims, barriers in public institutions, etc.) and in intersubjective terms (relationships with white Danes/Quebeckers, internalisation of inferiority, etc.).

I follow here Weheliye's approach, which, although drawing on poststructuralist theory, introduces the idea that people experiencing dehumanisation and political oppression are not necessarily defined by these experiences but rather find ways of circumventing, undermining, and dismissing such political oppression, demonstrating the power of hope—and possibly the agentic components of hope. The young Muslims I met in Montreal and Copenhagen were not consumed by their experiences of Islamophobia and racism; these experiences were often a backdrop to their lives in general. This is perhaps because the cohort of participants I met were socioeconomically secure, socially mobile, and often national citizens. In other words, they could navigate both the political and urban landscape with an ease of mind that, no matter their political exclusion, they had legal status, financial security, and social position.

Drawing on Stuart Hall and Spivak among others, Weheliye's approach utilises assemblages as relational connectivity across social entities. Anything that can be interconnected can become part of an assemblage: human, non-human, objects, discourses, spaces, etc. Racialisation processes are complex because of this interplay between a wide range of social entities. Assemblage theory as initially introduced by Delueze and Guettari tried to counter the hierarchical perspectives of poststructuralists, like Foucault, by introducing a non-hierarchical conceptualisation of society. Weheliye merges the two approaches by acknowledging the role that power dynamics play in assemblages. However, power dynamics are here understood as one of

26 *Muslim Racialisation and its Affects*

many entities rather than an all-encompassing structural phenomenon. In this sense, he demonstrates how the power of the state/nation or political violence/oppression is rarely all-consuming of people's lives. There are ways of creating assemblages away from and parallel to experiences of racism/nationalism/state oppression.

It is useful to include Jasbir Puar's (2013, 2018) approach to assemblages to Weheliye's framework. The way Puar approaches assemblages forces us to move away from binary assumptions about social positions and categories and allows us to conceive of various other formations of interconnectedness. With this approach, she builds on Kimberle Crenshaw's (Crenshaw, 1990) concept of intersectionality, which focuses on the multiple levels of discrimination working-class Black women experience in the US, related to their race, gender, and class position. The idea of intersectionality helps us to consider the intersecting ways racialised populations experience discrimination. In the following quote, Puar unpacks the issues with intersectionality and assemblages, respectively, but then demonstrates how the two concepts can in fact complement each other:

> There are different conceptual problems posed by each; intersectionality attempts to comprehend political institutions and their attendant forms of social normativity and disciplinary administration, while assemblages, in an effort to reintroduce politics into the political, asks what is prior to and beyond what gets established. So one of the big payoffs for thinking through the intertwined relations of intersectionality and assemblages is that it can help us produce more roadmaps of precisely these not quite fully understood relations between discipline and control.
>
> (Puar, 2020)

Thus, by combining an intersectional approach to the concept of assemblages, we can understand the fluidity of racialisation processes as well as the social and spatial connections that are constructed through these processes. Drawing on both Weheliye and Puar's conceptualisations, the assemblage of Muslim racialisation involves several entities that all of which influence how Muslims are viewed and treated in societies. These include political, popular, and media discourses that dehumanise, otherise, and essentialise Muslims (e.g. political rhetoric, news media representation, popular images). They also include more materialistic expressions of access to resources (e.g. social policies, housing, jobs). Finally, they include social and spatial expressions where discourses and material discrimination may influence intersubjective relationships in everyday life. Nevertheless, it is within the social and spatial fields that Muslims can navigate and contest their racialisation. Muslims are able to navigate these assemblages to various degrees based on their intersecting identifications, including their class, gender, citizenship, visible Muslimness, and phenotypical signifiers. These identifications present different limitations and potentials for resisting their racialisation. What is important in the Quebec and Danish context is that these assemblages can

Assemblages of Muslim Racialisation 27

exist without ever explicitly recognising the processes that racialise Muslims, creating an illusion of colour blindness.

The rest of this chapter will attempt to make the racialisation processes of Muslims explicit by unpacking how Muslims navigate, evade, or challenge various assemblages of racialisation in social and urban spaces. While this chapter focuses on racialised assemblages, it should not undermine the other assemblages these young people are connected to that allow for a more complex appreciation of their different experiences.

Ripples of Racialisation

For over two decades, if not more, the hijab and niqab have often become the centre of political attention when discussing overt religious symbols in Quebec and Denmark with political demands to regulate Muslim women's dress. As such, the hijab and Muslim women's dress in general have been important aspects of racialising Muslims in political discourse. Hijab thus becomes an object Muslims, women in particular, have to engage with and respond to. Not only when interacting with non-Muslim society, but even internally within Muslim contexts (more on this in chapter 3). It is therefore not surprising that it was a prevalent symbol in the narratives of the young women I met, whether they wore hijab or not. The young men, on the other hand, did not experience the same kind of overt reification of their Muslimness based on their dress in political discourse. They did, however, face a different set of challenges related to the prevalent political suspect of the violent Muslim man (Bhattacharyya, 2009). These stereotypes of "violent Muslim men" meant that these young men invested time and effort in engaging and challenging these ideas through (1) benevolent responses to racialised expressions in everyday life and (2) treading carefully around these racialised images of the Dangerous Muslim Man/Oppressed Muslim Woman.

In general, both the young men and women often seemed to have to navigate the difficult terrain between respectability and their self-chosen Muslimness. In the Danish context, Musa, a young man working in the hotel business while finishing his university degree, explained,

> Initially, I try to indicate that I'm Muslim. So, if a colleague invites me to go to Christmas lunch or something else non-Islamic, I try to reject it in a subtle way [...]. A problem I often face because I work in a hotel: most receptionists are young women, so there's a chance of physical contact, for example shaking hands. So I usually use the line "I only shake hands with the old or ugly, and you're neither" – they take that pretty well.
>
> (Musa, Copenhagen)[1]

---

1 All quotes have been transcribed ad verbatim and Danish quotes have been translated into English.

28 *Muslim Racialisation and its Affects*

The symbolic gesture of shaking hands in Denmark has been a contested politicised marker of difference between "the white Danish us and the Muslim Other." It has been interpreted by politicians as a sign of disrespect of gender equality to the point that the now former Integration Minister, Inger Støjberg, passed it into law as part of the citizenship ceremony. In this regard, she argued,

> If you don't want to shake hands with the mayor [during the citizenship ceremony], it can be understood as a clear sign that you don't believe in gender equality. That's inherently why there are Muslims who don't want to shake hands with the opposite gender. So, I definitely think you can say that this is essential.
>
> (quoted in Olsen, 2018)

It is within this political backdrop that Musa attempts to negotiate his position. The only way to make it palatable to his white female colleagues is by being charming and attempting to flatter them. Racialisation processes as a political ploy thus become deeply entrenched into everyday interactions. In other words, political discourse influences the social field Musa must navigate. It influences not only Musa's way of interacting with his white female colleagues, but most likely also influences his colleague's ability to read his refusal to shake hands as a sign of Muslimness, and possibly even a Muslimness that oppresses women. The political racialisation of Muslim men as inherently oppressive paints the canvas of Musa's intersubjective engagement with his white colleagues. The assemblage here creates an interconnection between "Muslims opposing gender equality" (political discourse)—"Muslim Men" (social position)—"White Women" (social position). Musa, as a self-identifying Muslim man, has to navigate a cartography of racialisation created by political discourse and legislation that paints him as oppressive. His white female colleagues inhabit this same cartography, which Musa attempts to pre-empt any potential conflict through charm and humour. This interaction demonstrates the complex challenges that these young men face trying to navigate a system that vilifies them *a priory*.

Contrary to Musa's example of navigating the racialised assemblage as a perceived oppressive Muslim man, Muslim women had to navigate this assemblage as oppressed victims. This created a different dynamic, where instead of hesitation and fear of being perceived as violent, the young women experienced having to prove their independence and competencies. For instance, in the Quebec context, Leyla explained the struggle of dealing with assumptions of passivity because of her intersecting identifications as both Muslim and woman:

> I feel like [the more] you try to convince [people] that you're good enough] the more tired you get. Like, I do my best, and if they ask, I will prove [myself], but I don't need to prove without asking me …

Assemblages of Muslim Racialisation 29

Especially when you're already in a situation where you are [seen as] *soumise* [submissive].

(Leyla, Montreal)

In a similar way, Iman from Denmark explained how she often was put in a defensive position trying to challenge the preconceived image of the Oppressed Muslim Woman:

At the same time, I met resistance from the surrounding society saying I should take it [the hijab] off etc. "Tell your father you don't have to wear it!". I often felt defensive: "I actually have a free choice. No, my parents aren't strict or have high academic expectations of me, and no I will not be forced into a marriage." It required a lot of energy to continuously try to climb out of the box they put you in, especially in high school.

(Iman, Copenhagen)

Contrary to Musa's narrative, which reads as a careful navigation through a rigged terrain that assumes his potential for violence, these two young women had to stomp their way through the images of their oppression. Figuratively, climbing out of the box they are put it by insisting on their confidence, independence, and capabilities.

The final example I want to draw on is about a young man, Adam, who was raised Christian, born in Iran, and immigrated to Quebec with his family when he was a child. His case demonstrates how Quebec, as well as Denmark for that matter, is part of a wider global geo-political discourse on the threat of the Muslim. Adam explains that living in Iran during his early years exposed him to a Muslim environment, which meant that post-9/11 in Canada, he had a more nuanced understanding of Muslims:

Every time there was issues, especially obviously after September 11, everyone was talking about Islam, and so forth. My attitude was never the attitude of most people, whereas it's something foreign, they don't understand it so they kinda characterise it in different ways. Whereas for me, it was something I knew, you know, it's not "other" for me. And I would always find myself in a position of defending Islam and Muslims, and just, like, giving [Muslims'] side of the story even though I wasn't Muslim, you know, it was just normal. Like, I remember in Religion-class in high school, I got into this whole argument with the teacher because he was characterising [Islam] in a certain way, and I was like: "No, it's not like that, you're comparing it wrong", and I'm pretty sure he got the impression that I was Muslim. So, they started this whole "Dialogue with Muslims," and they were like: "You should come," but I was like: "But I'm not Muslim." It just kinda happened like that. And obviously, I looked Muslim, I was Persian, so there's a

30   Muslim Racialisation and its Affects

lot of associations for people to make. I just felt it was funny [...]. They would just assume I was Muslim because I looked the part, and I spoke out for it and I knew more about it than most people, so they just put me in that category and labelled me [...]. I just found it really funny, but it didn't make me angry, like: "How could you say that."

(Adam, Montreal)

Adam explains here how people in his school environment would often assume he was Muslim simply because of his ethnic origins and his opposition to post-9/11 negative stereotypes about Islam and Muslims. He indicates here the general tendency of conflating religious and ethnic identification, especially regarding Muslims in the Global North. This demonstrates how the ripples of racialised assemblages connect it beyond the national or even local level to global geopolitical connections of the "War on Terror." Furthermore, it connects the assemblage beyond the self-ascribed Muslim as the racialised Other to include the assumed-to-be Muslim Other.

Racialisation in Public Space and Counter-processes

In the above section, I unpacked how young Muslims in Copenhagen and Montreal experienced racialising discourse as a backdrop they had to be conscious of when interacting with white colleagues, teachers, and sometimes even friends. This backdrop affected them differently according to intersecting identifications, including but not limited to gender, class, migration background, ethnicity, and displays of religious symbols (note how such qualifiers complicate the racialisation assemblage). In the next section, I want to demonstrate the interconnectedness between racialisation discourses and how they are expressed through spaces.

The Interconnection between Racialisation Processes and Spatialisation

Understanding space as part of an assemblage is not really a new idea. In fact, many urban theorists make insinuations to assemblage theory in their relational approach to spaces. Doreen Massey (2013 [1994]), for instance, argues how space and place are intimately connected with social relations. Likewise, Henri Lefebvre (2014)[1974]) contends that social relations are the foundation of spatialisation—the production of space. Massey highlights how these ideas of connection have been well-developed by Marxist theorists who have demonstrated the relationality between space and class. In her book *Space, Place and Gender*, she builds on this literature (her own included) to emphasise the importance of understanding how gender and the construction of gender relations too are profoundly connected to space (Massey, 2013). While she indicates that race is another important social concept that needs to be explored in relation to space, she does not delve much further. Drawing on this idea of space as essential to understanding social categories and relations, I argue that there is a profound connection between space and the processes of racialisation. These processes

Assemblages of Muslim Racialisation 31

cannot be untangled from the construction of class and gender but must be understood within the intersection of these (Crenshaw, 2018).

Racialisation affects Muslims through their social interactions as well as their spatial experiences (Razack, 2002). In this sense, it becomes important to explore how identifications of "race"/ethnicity, class, gender, and, in this context, Muslimness influence each other in spatial terms (ibid. 15).

In the political discourses that fuelled the campaigns in Figures 1.1 and 1.2, the Muslim was the focal point. Consequently, Muslims are expected to demonstrate the state's definition of gender equality and other liberal values to avoid being seen as working against state values (Quebec) or be associated with what the Danish Conservative People's Party have named "Nazi-islamism." With these images, the Muslim becomes racialised as a symbol of cultural inferiority and a potential threat to the liberal secular state. Most people passing by the billboards in the Montreal metro station (Figure 1.1) or downtown Copenhagen (Figure 1.2) may not experience how space can become a place which (re)produces racialisation. However, for many Muslims—both those who are marked by religious signifiers and those who are not—such spaces become something they inevitably must navigate

Figure 1.1 "Church. Synagogue. Mosque. Sacred—Equality between men and women. The State's religious neutrality. All also sacred."—parti Quebecois (provincial government party in Quebec in 2013). National campaign billboard at a metro-station in downtown Montreal, advocating "The Charter of Values" (Bill 60) banning "ostentatious" religious symbols in public spaces.

32 Muslim Racialisation and its Affects

Figure 1.2 "Stop Nazi Islam ism"—Conservative People's Party 2015, National Election Campaign Billboard in Copenhagen. Photo Credit: Francis Dean/ Corbis News via Getty Images.

through. Navigation in this sense is about the creative ways they explain, contest, or even ignore these spatial signs of exclusion.

Muslims in Montreal and Copenhagen may not have had the political legitimacy or power to resist such political campaigns in any effective way. However, what if we revisit Mahmood's claims of agency here (see "Introduction"). By conceptualising agency as a capacity for action rather than direct resistance, the objective becomes to circumvent racialisation processes rather than the almost impossible task of dismantling it. This approach thus enables us to appreciate other avenues of reclaiming public space that does not necessarily intend to dismantle the power dynamic of the assemblage. It may in fact even reproduce reified symbols of Muslim racialisation. Nevertheless, in doing so, Muslims can insist on their right to the space. For instance, Figure 1.3 is taken from the Islamic Awareness Week at a university in Montreal, where people can try on the hijab:

It is important to mention that hijab was not worn by all female volunteers at the Muslim Student Association. Yet this stall was an important one during the controversy of "The Charter of Values" (Bill 60). The Charter attempted to prohibit hijab, and other "ostentatious" religious symbols in public spaces, supposedly to ensure secularity and gender equality. By actively reifying a symbol of Muslimness, which is a dominant image

Assemblages of Muslim Racialisation 33

Figure 1.3 Poster for the "Try on hijab" stand during a university's Islamic Awareness Week, Montreal.

of Muslim women in public consciousness, Muslim students were able to double down on the exclusionary discourse of Bill 60, which particularly disadvantaged hijab-wearing women. They invited onlookers to demonstrate acts of solidarity and allowed for connections and alliances to be articulated. Muslims reifying the hijab in this way is not without its consequences, but in doing so, they challenged the prescriptions of Muslim gender inequality that the government had implied during the public debate on Bill 60.

Figure 1.4 is an image from a public iftar dinner during Ramadan in Copenhagen. A Muslim charity (DM-Aid) hosted a public iftar which included a call to prayer (athan) and communal prayer (salah) on the square in front of Copenhagen City Hall in 2016. In similar ways as the IAW in Montreal, this iftar was a way to use a public space to establish Muslims' belonging to the city. While politicians have been arguing for Muslims' incompatibility with Danish national values, the iftar was a way to challenge this narrative representing Muslims as a visible part of the country's capital city.

These two examples demonstrate how racialised Others can use "public spaces as a way of making a claim to them, that they belong within this space" (Shortell & Brown, 2016). Caroline Knowles points out that race is a part of the texture of space; she continues, "space is in fact a composite, active, archive of politics and individual agency" (Knowles, 2003). The political campaigns, presented in the two political campaign posters, are physical

34 *Muslim Racialisation and its Affects*

Figure 1.4 Public iftar dinner during Ramadan at Copenhagen Town Hall Square, 2015, Copenhagen. Image reprinted with permission from the organisers at DM-Aid. Photo Credit: DM-Aid.

manifestations of racialising discourse taking over public space, and thus, space is co-opted into the assemblage of racialisation. Muslims' movements through such spaces—particularly hijab-wearing women—can be understood as their inevitable contestation of this racialisation and insistence on being part of this public space, regardless of racialising politics attempting to spatially otherise them. Young Muslims moved through such spaces consciously and deliberately—they invaded these spaces, in the words of Nirmal Puwar (Puwar, 2004)—thereby contesting the spatial exclusion. In fact, often, they had no choice; they could not avoid inhabiting these spaces, despite their hypervisibility. It is in unpacking such racialised dynamics within spatial interactions that we can appreciate the interconnection between space and racialised discourses.

Conclusion

Research on race and space has often been concerned with addressing socially constructed categories of difference. The focus has been mostly on class—being concerned with the intersections of economic and political power (Neely & Samura, 2011). This chapter has expanded on this literature by introducing a theoretical framework of racialisation assemblages, where space is one entity in a multitude of entities that affect racialisation processes. By comparatively drawing on ethnographic data from Copenhagen and Montreal, I argue that the concept of assemblages allows us to create more complex analyses of racialisation processes in colour-blind societies that do not recognise racism as part of a social system.

Exploring racialisation processes in both social *and* spatial terms helps us to unpack the different and interconnected experiences of these processes. How do social interactions create potentials for challenging or reproducing racialisation? And how do spaces become actors of racialisation, privileging some people over others, while also providing potential for resistance and counter-narratives? These have been the main questions of this chapter through which the theory of assemblages provides a fluid and complex framework for analysis of racialisation processes. Once we appreciate the interconnection between space and social life, we can appreciate how space is socialised through people's everyday movements, uses, and interactions in space. Spatialisation—the social production of space—thus becomes drawn into the assemblages of racialisation and imbued with racialised dynamics and negotiations. In other words, racialisation, social life, and spatialisation are part of the same assemblage and are thus interconnected processes.

2 Middle-Class Muslim Respectability in Copenhagen

For over two decades, political and media discourses about Muslims in Denmark have often focused on reinforcing a representation of Muslims as foreigners. Muslims are represented as foreigners in every sense of the word; they are phenotypically, culturally, linguistically, and religiously foreign to the Danish national imagination. In extension to this, there is a conflation of ethnic and religious categories in Danish public discourse, where immigrant/descendant=Muslim, which in turn influences securitisation, integration, and border policies and debates (Kublitz, 2010; Rytter & Pedersen, 2014). As I got to know the young Danish Muslims I met, I quickly realised that this discourse was something they all had to deal with in daily encounters. I became accustomed to how entrenched the representational discourse was in their lives. These 18- to 25-year-old Copenhagen Muslims came of age at a time when the Danish People's Party—a right-wing social-conservative party—grew from being an insignificant political actor to becoming the third largest governmental party. This chapter explores the experiences of young Danish Muslims, whose high degree of social mobility makes them a minority within the minority Muslim population in Denmark. They introduce us to the nuances of negotiating one's social position in a context that often overlooks their potential, achievements, and their sense of entitled national belonging to Denmark.

The Illusion of Danish Homogeneity

During my fieldwork in Montreal, "the Muslim community" was an important framework to understand the youth's social lives vis-à-vis their feelings of belonging to a religious group and the processes of religious groupness. However, among the Danish youth, the concept of "Muslim community" was almost non-existent. Young Muslims in Denmark would rarely refer to Danish Muslims as belonging to a *lokalsamfund* or *fællesskab* (the two closest translations to community). This is an important distinction between the social framing of young people in Copenhagen and Montreal, which lies within the different national models of Canada and Denmark. The Canadian national image of a culturally diverse society constructed around the old multicultural idea of a national mosaic of smaller ethnic, migrant, language,

DOI: 10.4324/9781003294696-4

Middle-Class Muslim Respectability in Copenhagen   37

religious, or social communities is transferred into citizens' own sense of belonging. Young people in Quebec saw themselves as part of Canadian society simultaneously with being part of a Muslim community—nothing in their narratives of belonging challenged the national image of Canadian cultural diversity. Danish Muslims, on the other hand, faced the challenge of a national image of sameness as the cohesive factor connecting Danish society (Hervik, 2004; Jenkins, 2011; Olwig & Pærregaard, 2011).

The strong capitalist growth in Denmark in the last century was coupled with a strong welfare model that sought to create less distinct class-based differentiation between citizens. This welfare model was established around the idea of the Danish *Gemeinschaft* (Tonnies & Loomis, 2002), representing Denmark as a *community*—with the illusion of all its inhabitants knowing and sharing the same lifestyle—rather than the more socially detached *society*. My Danish interlocutors seemed to experience a challenge in this conflation of concepts. They would all argue to be Danish citizens doing their best to contribute to Danish society. However, they all struggled in different ways with the cultural framework of sameness they felt the Danish national image was based upon.

Rytter and Pedersen (2014) provide a detailed overview of the development in recent decades of negative political sentiments towards immigrants in general, and Muslims in particular. They argue that Danish political and media discourses represent a major but gradual shift in the representation of immigrants in public life over the past three decades that has normalised an integration and securitisation paradigm, where immigrants and Muslims are perceived as a quintessential "Other." Rytter and Pedersen explain that during the 1990s, there was a rise in cultural anxiety which was especially connected to a globalising economy, the European Union, and other signs of globalisation. This cultural anxiety was personified in the ethnic and religious minority population who were seen as "potential 'enemies within'" (Grillo, 2003, p. 2312). The result was that Anders Fogh Rasmussen, the Danish Prime Minister in the early 2000s, instigated what he called a cultural war (*kulturkamp*), a battle of cultural values, which sought to challenge immigrants' culture, religions, and lifestyles as inherently incompatible with Danish values (Grillo, 2003). This was a push towards the normalisation of a racialising rhetoric among both politicians and the news media. The Conservative Minister of Culture in 2005, Brian Mikkelsen, argued that there was a need to challenge immigrants who insisted on practising their "medieval norms" (Kublitz, 2010, p. 112). Not long after this shift in political rhetoric towards a "battle of values" (ibid.), the infamous cartoon crisis was initiated by a newspaper editor commissioning cartoonists to depict Prophet Mohammed, one of whom depicted the Prophet as a terrorist, in the name of upholding the ideal of freedom of speech (Henkel, 2010; Kublitz, 2010).

Prime Minister Fogh's shift in political focus from the traditional liberal centrist position of his *Venstre*-party towards a more right-wing approach of "protecting" Danish values meant an increased focus on immigrant and

38   *Muslim Racialisation and its Affects*

religious minorities' (mainly Muslims and people from the Global South) differences. Since the turn of the 21st century, there has thus been an increased political focus on "Danish values." This focus on Danish *common* values is not only driven by the political right but spans the spectrum of Danish political parties (ibid.). The focus on common values is based on the quest to maintain a "social cohesion" [*sammenhængskraft*] in the "Danish community" [*det danske fællesskab*] (Rostbøll, 2010, p. 392). The connotations of Denmark as a tightknit community are reflected in many of the discursive symbols used in political rhetoric. In these, Denmark is represented as homogenous, and the Danish people as sharing the same social and cultural values forming the basis of the welfare state. For instance, the employment minister in 2014, Mette Frederiksen, who later became prime minister (2019-2025) and is a member of the Social Democrats [*Socialdemokratiet*], at the time of my fieldwork established a new *Fællesskabspris* [Community Award] based on the idea that what makes Denmark great is the notion of a close-knit national community that seeks to take care of each other:

> What is special about Denmark is what we share. Our social security system, our good jobs, our free and equal access to education and health – our absolute trust and respect for each other. Have you considered that every time you get on the train, it's only possible thanks to the work of hundreds of men. What we take for granted in everyday life does not come out of the blue. The society that we Danes are rightly proud of, is the result of caring about each other – we want to engage with each other and carry the [social] burden together. An old proverb says, "that when two Danes meet, they shake hands. When three Danes meet, they form an association."
>
> (Frederiksen, 2014, translated from Danish)

In this quote, Frederiksen paints a romanticised picture of the Danish *Gemeinschaft*. It is not an impersonal society where citizens do not care about one another. Rather, by sharing the same values and social ideals, Danes want to feel close to their fellow citizens. As I have already noted, this imagery is recurrent in Danish political rhetoric across the ideological spectrum.

However, in its idealisation of the homogenous community, this national image reinforces a notion of a strong communal (white) "us" versus the different (racialised) "other." This "other" is often represented as people who do not share the same social, cultural, and religious values as the "Danish community."

A consequence of this "raceless" colour-blind yet implicitly racialised national(ist) rhetoric is that the racism and Islamophobia expressed in political rhetoric and news media have become commonsensical. This commonsense has seeped into everyday life to such a degree that many of my interlocutors could not avoid encountering various degrees of liberal racism,

Middle-Class Muslim Respectability in Copenhagen 39

often questioning their belonging and rootedness to Denmark. These young Muslims applied different tactics for dealing with such experiences in different contexts. For instance, one young man, Khalid, responded to a supervisor's apprehension and prejudice against him as a Muslim man by overcompensating with cordiality:

> You have to build relationships, and that's what I did with my [supervisor]. Initially, she didn't like me and didn't want to hire me [after my internship], but I made a good impression and was open with her, when we spoke about our private life, so they also know that you're a person. The [supervisor] definitely had her prejudice that had to be taken down slowly.
>
> (Khalid, Copenhagen)

He needed to break down her prejudice, because as a supervisor, she was a gatekeeper to securing a job. In another instance in his childhood, he responded more confrontationally, because there were fewer repercussions for his livelihood: "I speak better Danish than you do," he once told a white Danish man from rural South Jutland who complimented his Danish language proficiency. In most instances, the young people I met from Denmark struggled with calling out implicit forms of racism and Islamophobia that were never pronounced and could easily be dismissed by the perpetrators as non-intentional. Nevertheless, these instances reproduced hierarchies between white *real* Danes and racialised Others.

Political and media discourses and the national imagination of the "Danish community" are an essential background for understanding my interlocutors' experiences of growing up in Denmark post-9/11 era. The following cases explore how these young Muslims perceive and navigate through a social landscape that excludes them from the "Danish community"—how have these youth responded, ignored, or dealt with these feelings of exclusion?

Contextualising Racialisation in Denmark

When exploring the phenomenological experiences of young Muslims, we cannot disconnect these experiences from the structural realities that privilege white Danishness (Andreassen & Vitus, 2016; Gullestad, 2002; Hervik, 2019). Such nationalism is not merely a question of white Danes' treatment of minorities; rather, it is ingrained across Danish social structures, from laws privileging single citizenship to housing policies discriminating against citizens with non-Western ancestry (Freiesleben, 2016; Hervik, 2019; Rytter, 2010; Wren, 2001). My participants' knowledge of these structures—and how they play out in everyday life—is what enabled them to contest, challenge, and navigate through such interactions. Despite this reality, Danish political discourse readily draws upon racist tropes. For example, it is common to hear that Muslim men are more violent/criminal and Muslim women

40 *Muslim Racialisation and its Affects*

require progressive liberation (Razack, 2004). In fact, in her Parliamentary opening speech in 2020, Prime Minister Mette Frederiksen explicitly drew on such racist tropes:

> One in five young men of non-Western background, born in 1997, had transgressed the law, before he turned 21 years old. One in five. It is not all—definitely not all. But it is clearly too many. Young men, who take other's freedom, steal children's futures, break down prison guards— and leave a long trail of unsafety.
>
> (Frederiksen, 2020)

Frederiksen is here propagating an image of racialised young men as potentially dangerous. She is not the first to do so. In fact, it is a longstanding racist trope that has contributed to the fact that descendants of immigrants are 45% more likely to be charged by police without conviction than white Danes (The Danish Institute for Human Rights, 2022).

The Danish youth I spoke with were well-aware of the existing power dynamics that political and media rhetoric emphasised through their discourse of the inferior and potentially dangerous Other. Our conversations often led back to the question of representing "the good/respectable Muslim": a productive, successful citizen that is both Muslim and Danish. Mahmood Mamdani (2005) has argued that the "Good Muslim/Bad Muslim" dichotomy is a result of the War on Terror's moral dictum; the idea that you are either with us (i.e. the West) or against us. However, Danish Muslims' performances of the good or respectable Muslim do not necessarily refer to this moral dictum. In fact, the youth did not hesitate to be openly Muslim and defiant of social expectations, i.e. requesting a prayer space at school or work or wearing hijab or jilbab (long Arabic dress) in professional settings. Several young Muslims described how, if they were contributing members of Danish society, they were entitled to inhabit its spaces, including expressing their religiosity in public. These youth were thus not necessarily submissive to white hegemonic demands of assimilation. Rather, they were savvy enough to know how to navigate a field rigged against them and how to get the best out of it, as Khalid explains in the following when responding to my question about facing prejudice.

> You're not like everyone else in Denmark, and you have to remember you're Muslim first and foremost, and you should show your best qualities, because then you can't fail – to display good manners and *akhlaq* [character].
>
> (Khalid, Copenhagen)

What Khalid is indicating here is that to him, representing respectability is connected to his Muslimness, which in turn enables him to contest the racialisation of Muslims. In other words, these middle-class Muslim's politics of respectability cannot necessarily be disconnected from their religiosity. The following paragraph unpacks this in more detail by referring back to Evelyn Brooks Higginbotham's original concept of respectability politics and its connection to the Black church movement in the US.

Politics of Respectability

To unpack the interrelation between racialisation and class dynamics among Muslims, I am inspired by Evelyn Brooks Higginbotham's (1993) conceptualisation of the politics of respectability. Higginbotham's analysis of respectability politics is based on her feminist history of Black Baptist women's activism within the church congregation at the turn of the 20th century US. In her book *Righteous Discontent* (1993), she contends that at a time of Jim Crow laws, lynching of Black people and general inferiorisation of the Black population in the US, these black women traversed a complex field of performing white middle-class respectability while at the same time working for the advancement of lBack people's rights. Respectability politics, or rather the critique of performing respectability to appease the white gaze, has since been oft critiqued in both academic and activist circles. Although this critique is highly valuable in unpacking how to resist white supremacy and assimilationist rhetoric, it misses out on an important point of Higginbotham's argument. Throughout her analysis, Higginbotham does not necessarily rebuke these women's respectability performances but rather demonstrates how these performances were a way to open a window for their demands for fair treatment of Black people in all aspects of society, from Black neighbourhood infrastructure to access to education. The politics of respectability was thus not simply bad politics of reproducing the inferiorisation of Blackness in white supremacist US, but rather a way to navigate a racialisation that impeded every aspect of societal life for Black people. These women were not necessarily politically powerful, nor even particularly wealthy, as other Black communities that Higginbotham refers to. Rather, they were first-generation labourers, but through their lobby work and local community mobilisation, they advanced the Black cause and, according to Higginbotham, were the precursors to the Black civil rights movement of the 1960–1970s.

Building on Higginbotham's concept, but within a French context looking at French middle-class Muslims, Margot Dazey (2021) emphasises the complexity of the politics of respectability. It is not about reproducing white hegemonic values, but rather should be understood at the conjunction between practices of resistance and practices of discipline. She suggests that respectability politics is a way to both counter negative representations and gain (presumably white) social acceptance. The politics of respectability is thus reactive, in the sense that it is a response to suspicion and marginalisation from broader society and public institutions. It is a way of disciplining "speeches, gestures, clothing, and postures, and to coerce bodies into compliance with social norms" (Dazey, 2021, p. 582).

42 *Muslim Racialisation and its Affects*

While respectability politics might be a reaction to racist and Islamophobic discourse among middle-class Danish Muslims similar to the French case, I argue we should move away from the nexus of resistance and discipline. This formulation relies too much on the resistance/subordination dichotomy that Saba Mahmood critiques in *Politics of Piety* (2004), which I discussed in the Introduction. Danish Muslims are rather applying whatever capacity they have to act within a social context that assumes their inferiority. Consequently, they seem less focused on calling out racism, discrimination, and Islamophobia. Instead, these young adults are more focused on figuring out how to navigate a field that is full of misgivings and suspicion, maybe even an expectation that these youth should prove their worth (through studiousness, work effort, attitude, etc.) before acknowledging their right to belong. The young people I met in Copenhagen came of age in socially stigmatised neighbourhoods and felt a need to highlight their academic and professional successes, working their way up from working-class families to a middle-class position. Contrary to many racialised minorities in Denmark, who have historically belonged to a working underclass, my interlocutors represented a privileged group of young, highly educated, and professionally successful racialised citizens. This provided them a unique opportunity to challenge racist rhetoric, especially those attempting to limit their self-expressions as Danish Muslims. Furthermore, their social capital allowed them to resist stereotypes of the inferior Muslim Other by emphasising their success as well as their belonging to Denmark as Muslims rather than as Others because of their Muslimness.

Danish Muslims as Non-Westerners

In 2017, a broad majority of the government coalition parties (mainly right-wing, conservative, and centrist parties) voted to continue to limit asylum from what the government has categorised as non-Western countries[1]. The political rhetoric that accompanied this Parliamentary decision was largely based on promoting a fear that white Danes had become a minority in some residential neighbourhoods with many immigrants and descendants of immigrants (Folketinget, 2017).

---

1 Non-Western countries include all countries in Africa; South and Central America; Asia; all countries in Oceania (except Australia and New Zealand); Albania; Bosnia-Hercegovina; Belarus; Yugoslavia; Kosovo; Macedonia; Moldova; Montenegro; Russia; Serbia; Soviet Union; Turkey; and Ukraine; as well as stateless individuals (Danmarks Statistik, https://www.dst.dk/da/Statistik/dokumentation/hvadbetyder#). In 2020, the non-Western category was categorised further, distinguishing immigrants and descendants from Middle East, North Africa, Pakistan, and Turkey (MENAPT) from the broader category of non-Westerners (Denmark: New statistics category for migrants from Muslim countries | European Website on Integration (europa.eu).

Middle-Class Muslim Respectability in Copenhagen   43

The phrasing of Danes versus descendants of non-Western immigrants became the focus of attention in the ensuing media debate. The Parliament's statement thus became the most recent explicit differentiation between white Danes and racialised Others. This legal categorisation classifies descendants of non-Western immigrants as non-Danes because of their supposed lack of cultural similarity to white Danes. This Parliament statement is just the most recent version that enforces an "us vs them" dichotomy in a long line of different racialising concepts that have normalised an assimilationist paradigm in everyday life through which young Muslims have to navigate. The following ethnographic cases demonstrate different ways these youth negotiate their social position as racialised Others.

Negotiating Social Position

Experiencing Racialisation in Everyday Life

Aisha was a 22-year-old woman born and raised in Denmark. Her grandfather, a tailor, came to Copenhagen in the 1970s as a guest worker. Aisha and her siblings were all born and raised in a borough not far from downtown Copenhagen. Aisha's description of her upbringing is imbued with considerable fondness for her parents and family. Her father especially demonstrated to her the importance of standing up for one's rights and was an important role model for Aisha in the face of racism and discrimination.

When I met Aisha, she was finishing her undergraduate studies in a highly competitive field and planning to continue with postgraduate studies. Aisha represents a minority of descendants of immigrants in Denmark who have achieved an upward social mobility through higher education (Dahl & Jakobsen, 2005). Their parents or grandparents were often unskilled immigrant workers from the Global South (although in Aisha's case, her grandfather was a professional tailor). These workers migrated to Denmark under the "guest worker" scheme in the 1960s and 1970s. Although highly educated descendants of migrants, such as Aisha, are still a minority, the number of descendants achieving higher professional salaries have increased by 30% in recent years (2010–2014) according to Statistics Denmark (*Danmarks Statistik*) (Christensen & Stræde, 2016). Aisha and the other young people I met in Denmark were too young to be represented in this statistic that focuses on salaries earned after completing one's degree. Nonetheless, all my interlocutors had finished at least secondary school and all of them were either already enroled in higher education or were planning to take a gap-year. Aisha's case illustrates the experiences of achieving social mobility while still experiencing the effects of dominant discourses of racialising Muslims as Other and not belonging to Danish society.

Aisha went to a Muslim private school for her primary school education, but switched to the Danish public school system for her secondary schooling. It was not until she made the switch to a Danish high school that she first

44 *Muslim Racialisation and its Affects*

experienced the effects of otherisation. The high school had a few Muslim students though, so Aisha never felt completely estranged. Aisha describes her sentiments in the following conversation I had with her:

> I always feel like you're judged, you're always judged. I've also experienced it in high school. I once had a really big discussion with people. I never expected to discuss these things with [my friend], we never spoke about immigrants or ethnic minorities. My cohort in high school, half were "new Danes", or whatever you want to call it, I don't like these terms.
> *What would you call it?*
> Danes. Dark-skinned Danes. Half were dark-skinned, and half were not. One day we were talking about our graduation trip [*studenterkørsel*] and alcohol etc. And then one of my really good white, or light-skinned, Danish friends said: "Well listen, you guys are also [just] immigrants" and stuff like that. I was just like: "Wait a minute, I'm not an immigrant. You have to know my history before you talk! My grandfather was a guest worker, there's a big difference. We're neither refugees nor immigrants. Yes, we migrated, but even an international student is an immigrant here". Anyway, then I told her: "Listen, my grandfather, he was a tailor, he was a guest worker, he had his own shop right here on [a street in Copenhagen], so I don't know what you're talking about! The fact that he got his family sponsored, was an offer from Denmark, it wasn't something he himself had gotten. So, they [Denmark] actually invited my grandmother and my family. So, I don't know what you're talking about. I'm just as Danish as you are, just in a different way." So, I was very, I actually felt really hurt that people would call me.
> *I think it's interesting that you define it as: "We're all Danes, there's just some who are a bit darker skinned than others." Do you think your friend, did she characterise you as an immigrant because of your darker skin or because you're Muslim?*
> Because I'm Muslim. Because if I did what they did, she wouldn't have discussed this with me, [i.e.] the fact that I'm immigrant. Especially because I'm not that much darker skinned. I could look Brazilian, Latin American, but I know this for a fact that it's because I'm Muslim and covered [wearing the hijab]. The more practising you are, the more "immigrant" you are, if you can say it that way. That's how I feel.
>
> (Aisha, Copenhagen)

This lengthy excerpt highlights several issues that are pertinent to the "host vs guest"-discourse about immigration and Muslims that I referred to earlier. Aisha explained her frustration with having to clarify to others—even close friends—the distinction she made between being a Danish Muslim and being an immigrant. Aisha stressed her Danishness in the argument with her friend,

Middle-Class Muslim Respectability in Copenhagen   45

and thus objected to the invalid representation of her as an immigrant, i.e. a "guest" that needed to conform to the Danish way of doing things. She thus argued against cultural conformity as a way of determining Danishness and instead emphasised her own sense of national belonging. She highlighted the uniqueness of her family's migration story, challenging the homogenising discourse on migrants—her grandfather was a professional tailor, her family was *invited* by the Danish state—and thereby stressing her entitlement to Danishness.

Speaking against the "us vs them" dichotomy, Aisha was explicit in voicing her dislike of the term "new Danes." The concept of "new Danes" is fairly recent and is often used interchangeably for both new immigrants who have recently acquired their citizenship as well as migrant descendants. "New Danes" evolved to distinguish immigrants and descendants, who had been Danish citizens for decades or even born as citizens, from white Danes. The term "new Dane" has thus become another form of categorical distinction, which connotes difference and marginality from wider society (Dastageer, 2013). Since 2017, however, the term used in political rhetoric as well as policies has been "non-Western immigrants and descendants," thus re-enforcing a differentiation between people of colour and white citizens (i.e. Westerners). Aisha displayed the discursive effects of this problematic categorisation when she struggled to find the right terms to differentiate between white Danes and racialised Danes.

In a dominant discourse that associates *difference* with *inferior*, any other term than "Dane" is problematic. Aisha's description of a white Danish friend in high school, who had used the word "immigrant" in a derogatory way, demonstrates her friend's frustrations with Muslim classmates who did not want to join the graduation festivities (driving around Copenhagen in a party truck) because of the alcohol consumption that is traditionally an important part of these celebrations. Aisha showcased how her friend was hinting that Muslims were in fact *not* "Danish, but rather "immigrants," because of their Muslimness. Aisha quickly reacted to her friend's "accusation" by stating that in fact, she "is not an immigrant," and provided a more detailed description of her family's migration history. It is significant to note that Aisha immediately picked up on her friend's racist insinuation of the immigrant label. Aisha understood the implicit differentiation between ethnic Danes and Danish citizens who are deprived of their *social* citizenship because of their cultural difference. She therefore responded by forcefully opposing the immigrant label as it connoted someone who does not belong to Danish society.

At the end of this excerpt, Aisha clarified that her white friend categorised her as an immigrant not because of her family's migration history but because of her Muslim lifestyle that prevented her from engaging in certain social activities. Later in the interview, she elucidated this point further when comparing herself with two white Christian classmates who also chose not to engage in the same activities because of religious concerns. While her choices

46 *Muslim Racialisation and its Affects*

were considered "foreign," Aisha noted that her Christian classmates were not assigned such labels. She was frustrated with the difference in treatment. It highlighted to her how her Muslimness would always serve as a classification that excluded her from the Danish "us" category. Aisha's response demonstrates a contention towards being placed in a position of inferiority to white Danes in her class. Because Aisha saw herself as a Danish Muslim, she resisted her friend's pressure to conform to certain conventions. She retorted that she was "just as Danish [...], just in a different way".

Experiencing Exclusion: "There's No Room for Me"

I have already briefly introduced Iman in Chapter 1, but here I will delve into more details on her experiences coming of age in Copenhagen. When I met her, Iman was 23 years old, and like Aisha, her family had lived in Denmark for many decades. Her mother was only 4 years old when Iman's grandparents immigrated to Copenhagen, and she enjoyed having a larger extended family in Denmark. Iman was newly married and lived in a small Copenhagen apartment. Her husband had recently graduated from university while she was finishing her final year of undergraduate studies. Iman's description of her family history in Denmark introduces the changing dynamics of immigration politics and their impact on young descendants.

Iman grew up in a disadvantaged borough of Copenhagen marked by low-income households, substance abuse, and other features of deprivation, though the area has been gentrified in recent years. She explained that her childhood memories of this neighbourhood were coloured by everyday discrimination. She would often receive discriminatory comments on the street from passersby:

> It's as if the ones that are struggling the most have the most difficulties with minorities. [...] I remember one experience with my mom and siblings: people on the bus commented that we were exploiting the system. Back then there were a lot of prejudice against women wearing the headscarf, so they were always shocked when my mom opened her mouth and spoke Danish fluently.
>
> (Iman, Copenhagen)

Iman explained that she understood the cause of discrimination in her neighbourhood. Poor white Danes struggling with their own disenfranchisement and marginalization used minorities as a scapegoat. However, in this quote Iman recalled one incident of racist verbal abuse clearly: the bullies were surprised by her mother's fluency in Danish, thinking she would not understand their offensive commentary. A racialised stereotype of Muslim migrants and their descendants lingers and often portrays them as lacking integration into Danish language and culture.

Middle-Class Muslim Respectability in Copenhagen   47

The discrimination Iman experienced was especially directed towards her choice to differentiate herself from white Danes by wearing the hijab from a young age. The hijab became a representation of cultural distinction and was therefore often perceived as connoting a lack of integration.

> At the same time, I met resistance from the surrounding society saying I should take it [the hijab] off etc. "Tell your father you don't have to wear it!". I often felt defensive: "I actually have a free choice. No, my parents aren't strict or have high academic expectations of me, and no I will not be forced into a marriage." It required a lot of energy to continuously try to climb out of the box they put you in, especially in high school.
>
> (Iman, Copenhagen)

Revisiting this quote that I introduced in Chapter 2, it is clear how Iman's hijab became a representation of "foreignness" that resisted conforming to Danish normativity. Iman herself was treated as a representation of the Muslim female stereotype: presumed to be oppressed by a patriarch, with no freedom to choose her lifestyle. Iman would retort that her religious lifestyle choices were her own. Her defensive insistence on her lifestyle being an autonomous choice rather than a result of family pressure highlights the social pressure she felt to challenge the stereotypes of Muslim descendants. If she could not live up to the imagined Danish homogeneity, she could at least defend her choice by claiming autonomy from her family. She could thus argue against the stereotype of immigrant parents' social control of their children, *pressuring* them to live a particular social, cultural, and religious lifestyle that conforms with their "countries of origin."

Following my fieldwork trip in December 2013, the Integration Minister, Anette Vilhelmsen (at the time a member of the left-leaning Social People's Party, *SF*), initiated a PR campaign that sought to elevate awareness about and eliminate Muslim parents' "social control" over their children's lifestyles. This "social control" was represented as the parents' way of pressuring their children to wear hijab, achieve higher academic degrees, not drink alcohol, or have premarital sexual relationships, etc. (Vilhelmsen, 2013). Political and media discourses (across the political spectrum) about Muslim parents' social control that arose since this campaign was initiated, basically questions every decision that someone like Iman, as a young Muslim *woman*, makes, whether it is a religious, social, or cultural lifestyle choice.

The questions Iman faced regarding her parents' level of "social control" may not always have been ill-intentioned but may also have been an expression of genuine concern for Iman's ability to make free lifestyle choices. Yet, these concerns always came off as an offensive and racist denunciation of Iman's family relationships, which she highlighted were based on encouragement and respect. Thus, Iman experienced these encounters with concerned white Danes as racism based on her Muslimness and ethnicity. She felt she

48   Muslim Racialisation and its Affects

was not being judged fairly based on her abilities but rather based on her ethnicity and lack of Danishness. As she explained:

> I became bitter. It was a negative energy. I started to understand those troublemakers in *Nørrebro* [a neighbourhood district in Copenhagen] who face so much resistance that they chose the streets instead of school. To be told that you'll never be able to achieve this or that, you can never be as good at [speaking] Danish, your religion is old-fashioned, your culture doesn't belong. [...] I started to become bitter, and anti-Denmark. [...] A couple of years ago during the riots [by young men of immigrant descent] in Denmark, [Prime Minister Anders] Fogh said: "*We* don't do that in Denmark", but those troublemakers don't know anything but Denmark, why make it an 'Us vs Them'- question?
>
> (Iman, Copenhagen)

During Iman's high school years, the debates that surfaced in the media regarding Muslims and immigrants were not something she could simply tune out. During the early 2000s, there was an increased political focus on Danish values vis-à-vis immigrants (particularly Muslim immigrants), which increased the news media's focus on issues related to Danes versus immigrants (including second- and third-generation descendants). The comments that Iman is referring to from the former Danish Prime Minister, Anders Fogh Rasmussen (2001–2009), focusing on this dichotomy, highlights a "host vs guest" discourse which presumes that immigrants and their descendants should simply be grateful to live in Denmark (Hervik, 2004).

During her high school years, Iman felt the effects of such exclusionary discourse, and the prejudice she experienced affected her attitude towards Danish society in general. She clarified that although she did have friends who were not Muslim, none of them were white Danes. Iman's friendships reflected the ethnocentric divide she experienced in her interactions with white people through her school environment. This ethnocentrism was further exacerbated by the political climate of the years she came of age post-9/11. This climate had disregarded young Muslims' experiences of systemic discrimination, e.g. in employment, schools, and community-organisations (Dahl & Jakobsen, 2005; Larsen, 2000). In a speech delivered at the 2005 Conservative National Conference, the Conservative Culture Minister, Brian Mikkelsen, highlighted this distinction by undermining the legitimacy of Danish Muslims' lifestyles:

> We have also been fighting against the multicultural ideology that says everything is equally good. Because if everything is equally good, then everything does not matter. And we will not accept that.
>
> A medieval Muslim culture will never be as valid at home [i.e. Denmark] as the Danish culture, which has grown from this piece of

Middle-Class Muslim Respectability in Copenhagen   49

old soil that lies between Skagen and Gedser and between Dueodde and Blåvandshuk [Danish towns].

The battle of culture and values has been raging for some years now. And I think we can declare that the first part [of the battle] is about to be won.

(Mikkelsen, 2005)[2]

As a reaction to this political rhetoric and its expression in her everyday high school interactions, Iman insisted on emphasising her Moroccan background. She highlighted to her classmates the fact that it was not her choice to be born in Denmark. So, if her lifestyle was perceived as "too foreign" for Danish standards, she did not perceive herself as Danish anyways. Iman's choice to underline her ethnic difference arose as a particular response to her perception of the exclusivity with which Danishness was being constructed. In other words, if Iman could not be perceived as Danish because of her Muslim lifestyle, it was not worth fighting for the label.

> In high school, I insisted on being Moroccan, but when I travelled to Morocco I realized I'm not Moroccan in the least. I'm a product of Denmark, and I couldn't imagine living anywhere else. […]It is a fixed mindset that dominates Danes a lot, but I don't feel it in my everyday life. I choose not to keep up with politics, it makes me too frustrated. Everything that is about being Danish in public space I don't interfere with. I keep my Danishness *[Danskhed]* at home, my ryebread, my *koldskål* [vanilla-buttermilk dessert], I laugh at my Danish movies, I live in Denmark, but everything else I don't get involved in, because there's no room for me.
>
> (Iman, Copenhagen)

It is interesting to note that in this quote, Iman acknowledges that she was more Danish than she cared to admit during her high school years. She insisted, however, on keeping her Danishness private. It was not something to be discussed; if national(ist) political discourse could not acknowledge her Danishness because of her ethnicity or Muslimness, she would eat her ryebread and watch her Danish movies in private.

Most of my other interlocutors followed Aisha's example: they felt entitled to define themselves as Danish Muslims and negotiated their claim to be regarded as Danes in different ways through their everyday lives in Copenhagen. Iman, however, did not care to get involved in the debate with white Danes in her daily life. Iman was born and raised in Denmark by parents and grandparents who had lived in Denmark for most of their lives, and Copenhagen was therefore undeniably her home. It was redundant for her to

2 Translated from Danish.

50   Muslim Racialisation and its Affects

even argue the question of her belonging to Denmark. It was simply a matter of fact. The political rhetoric had done its part in normalising the integration-paradigm that enforced the idea that Muslim immigrants and their descendants still had to integrate into Danish society by adopting "Danish values" (Rytter & Pedersen, 2014). While Iman protested this integration-paradigm by understating her own feelings of Danishness, many of my interlocutors often got swept away by defensiveness when facing such demands of integration, which they eagerly tried to challenge it by insisting on being respectable *Danish* Muslim.

It is telling to juxtapose Iman's experiences with her mother's experiences when the family first arrived in Denmark during the 1970s:

> Now, I have a very "Danish" mom. We usually tease her by calling her Pernille. Her life in Denmark is completely different from mine. While I was a bitter teenager, she was a hippie- Dane. When she describes her childhood when she came with her parents as a four-year-old, she describes how she would sit on the bus and people wanted to touch her curls, and: "Wow, how beautiful you are". And Danish friends is something completely natural to her, she has a lot of those, even today. Yeah, I had Danish friends, but their parents were so scared: "Be careful" [their parents would tell their children]. They weren't allowed to eat at our place. So, my whole life I've had friends that weren't ethnic Danes. My mother experienced it differently.
>
> (Iman, Copenhagen)

Iman explained how her mother's and her own experience in interacting with Danish society were almost contradictory. Her quote highlights the temporality of political discourse and media-perpetuated stereotypes. When her mother first came to Denmark as a young girl in the 1970s, a more neutral discourse about immigrants existed among the general public with little public concern about issues arising from increased immigration (Goul, 2002, p. 12). Jørgen Goul argues that statistically, Danes were more hostile towards immigrant cultures in the 1970s compared to similar quantitative studies conducted in the 1990s. Yet, because of the lack of political and media attention, the Danish public was simply not interested in immigration issues (Goul, 2002).

Immigrants in the 1960s–1970s were "guest workers" who were helping rebuild Danish society in the post-World War II period, and they were expected to return to their countries of origin at one point (Olwig & Pærregaard, 2011, p. 12). In other words, because immigrants were expected to be temporary, their different lifestyles were not seen as a threat to Danishness unlike more recent political representations. The exotic appearance and curly hair of Iman's mother, as she explained, were a source of positive distinction, rather than being signs of marginalised "otherness" and inciting feelings of resentment. Iman's mother therefore did not experience

Middle-Class Muslim Respectability in Copenhagen 51

the same discrimination because of the lack of public attention surrounding her cultural, ethnic, and religious differences. Her mother learnt to navigate Danish social space with ease. This was something Iman was deprived of growing up in a post-9/11 society.

Already in the early 1990s, Danish political rhetoric and immigration policies had changed dramatically, depicting immigrants and refugees as unemployed and unable (or unwilling) to integrate into Danish society (Yilmaz, 2016). These depictions of the "unintegrated immigrant" paid little attention to the social and economic structures within Denmark that enforced these "migrants" and "refugees" marginalisation (Olwig & Pærregaard, 2011, p. 13).[3] By the early 2000s, negative discourses against immigrants had increased dramatically and thus became Iman's predominant experience with Danish society.

Iman's narrative highlights an important perspective on how my Danish interlocutors respond to categorical representations and negative stereotypes. As I emphasised in Aisha's case, she insisted on the legitimacy of her Danishness while also being Muslim. This was her way of protesting representations of an exclusive Danish ethnonationalist identity. Iman, however, protested the discriminatory differentiation between the *real* Danes (i.e. white) and not-so-real ethnic minorities by renouncing her entitlement to the Danish category qua her citizenship. By choosing to highlight her ethnic and religious difference instead, she was able to resist being defensive about her non-conforming (and thus "un-Danish") lifestyle choices.

Gendered Perspectives

Muslims in Denmark are highly visible in the political and media discourse, and historically have been perceived as synonymous with immigrants and their descendants (going back two to three generations). Along these lines, Muslim women are often perceived as under the control of their patriarchal family and thus as submissive and oppressed (Razack, 2004). The stereotype of young Muslim men, on the other hand, focuses on their potential for aggressiveness and violence, either as criminals or potential radical terrorists (Bhattacharyya, 2009). In the Danish context, Fatima Al-Shamasnah and Jinan Hammoude (2023) demonstrate how negative gender stereotypes of Muslim men affect these men on an intersectional level based on their religion, ethnicity, and age. Their masculinity thus further marginalises them

---

3 The early immigrants were expected to be temporary migrants, and there were therefore no political initiatives to teach these immigrants Danish or include them in other welfare initiatives – that is until they started seeking reunification with their wives and children and became permanent migrants, who would need to use the Danish welfare system, e.g. schools, health care services, etc. (Rytter & Pedersen, 2014, p. 2310).

52   *Muslim Racialisation and its Affects*

within Danish society, and they must employ strategies to mitigate their experiences of marginalisation.

In many ways, it seemed relatively easier for Muslim women to contest stereotypes of submissiveness, especially given their social capital and academic achievements. Nevertheless, the young men I met in Copenhagen found creative strategies to contest the stereotypes of their latent aggressiveness. Like my female interlocutors, they all represented well-educated and socially mobile young Muslims born or raised in Denmark. However, while most of the female interlocutors did not invest much time in extracurricular sports during their younger years, several of my male interlocutors spent a lot of their time invested in local sports. These sports came to shape much of their youth and gave them critical resources and social capital with which to contest certain stereotypes. Focusing on two young men's experiences in the following, I make the argument that investing their time in local sports associations became a creative avenue for these youth to gain social capital and navigate a field that often undermined their potential.

Chess as a Tactic for Social Mobility

When I met Ahmad, he was 19 years old, born and raised in Copenhagen, and attending his first year of university. Growing up in a north-west suburb of Copenhagen, Ahmad grew up in a culturally diverse area. Like several other youth I spoke to, Ahmad went to a private Muslim primary school and switched to the public school system during his high school years. The youth who had attended Muslim primary schools seemed to all share the feeling of being sheltered from racism that they later experienced in secondary school. Ahmad, however, did not experience the same level of discrimination that some of my participants had. He described his high school experiences as positive. Ahmad was open about his religious principles when it came to avoiding socialising around drinking with his non-Muslim peers and he was quick to suggest alternative things to do, such as sports or going to the movies.

Ahmad focused on the positive aspects of growing up in Copenhagen, avoiding discussions of discrimination and racism. From the outset of our conversation, Ahmad mentioned in detail his active involvement in a national association that seeks to encourage children to play chess. Ahmad had positive encounters with white Danish peers and adults who shared his interests in chess outside of a school setting. He was introduced to the chess association when the general secretary recognised his enthusiasm for the game. The general secretary encouraged him to join the association to promote the game among other racialised youth:

> The general secretary from the association thought I was pretty good at the game and asked if I wanted to help promote [the chess association] with the sole purpose of showing ethnic diversity. I told him I could

Middle-Class Muslim Respectability in Copenhagen   53

understand that, then I said yes [to the invitation]. And then little by little I got more influence and became a member of their board in the [X] branch and was given the opportunity to make decisions. And later on, I was also allowed to participate in projects and help with that, and then I got the opportunity to become a member of the [X] board, and then … I know it's only chess, but it's actually a very big deal.

How has it influenced you?

With organizational work, how to … it's basic stuff, because I didn't know, I was a primary school student, [I didn't know] how to sit in a meeting with adults, how to reach a joint decision as a group, how to set deadlines, how to plan ahead, how to deal with unexpected factors that arise , how to be considerate of others' opinions. So, it did two things: it shaped me as a person and as a citizen. He [the general secretary] wanted, I think, to make sure I don't end up in a bad environment. Later, he got to know me very well and understood that I would never end up in those environments.

(Ahmad, Copenhagen)

From the way Ahmad described it, the general secretary seemed to have seen potential in Ahmad. The fact that Ahmad's school was located in an inner-city area that had in the past been close to neighbourhoods of high crime and gang activity seemed to have been a motivator for the general secretary to take Ahmad under his wing as a way of protecting him from that environment. Ahmad accepted the general secretary's offer to become a representative of ethnic minorities—literally a poster-child for diversity. However, he made sure to demonstrate through his work in the association that he was never an "at-risk-youth." He was regularly invited to municipality meetings with other local associations as he became older and started coaching chess in a local school. Ahmad described being introduced to a local soccer coach at one of these meetings. He explained that soccer and other sports played an even bigger role than chess when he was growing up, and thus when the local soccer coach offered him an assistant coach position, he was excited to accept. Ahmad highlighted this experience to underline the fact that being involved and engaged in local activities gave him experience in dealing with local authorities. In turn, it gave him the ability to navigate these social fields with ease, often bettering his social position through his involvements.

Throughout Ahmad's narrative, he demonstrated a certain degree of tactical skills in navigating the stereotype of young male migrant descendants that depicts him as a potential threat. Ahmad explained that he was invited to become an active part of Danish School Chess based on his immigrant descent and his enrolment in an inner-city school. While Ahmad did not himself see any racist elements in this categorisation—rather just well-intentioned support from someone in a position of authority—it is a consequence of a longstanding racialisation of young Muslim men in Denmark as potentially dangerous. This is the image, which most recently was promoted by the

54 *Muslim Racialisation and its Affects*

Prime Minister in 2020, which Ahmad and all the other Danish young men I spoke to had to navigate as they interact with people in positions of authority as well as everyday encounters with white Danes.

Being perceived as "at-risk" is a less charged categorisation than being seen as potentially dangerous. So instead of objecting from the outset to this categorisation, Ahmad wanted to represent Muslim private school in the chess association. As he progressed in the association, he eventually challenged the general secretary's assumption of being "at-risk." Simultaneously, he gained important social capital in how to deal with people with whom he did not necessarily have much in common outside of a particular activity. More importantly, he learnt how to engage with adults in a professional setting. This gave him confidence in local politics as he learnt to navigate the field of requesting municipality grants for community projects.

Ahmad's narrative exemplifies how being in close interaction with Danish associations from a young age allowed him to develop personal relationships with people in authority who also believed in his abilities and saw his potential beyond the racist stereotypes of racialised young men. These relationships became an important avenue for Ahmad to position himself as respectable. Perhaps more importantly, through this respectable positioning, he developed capabilities to navigate local authorities that in turn helped him get grants for his community projects. This is comparable to the main point Higginbotham makes about the politics of respectability. Ahmad may not actively resist the racist image of the racialised young man that the Danish Prime Minister promotes in her Parliamentary speech. Nevertheless, his respectability politics does create avenues for Ahmad to uplift his local community through sports grants and initiatives that support children from deprived neighbourhoods.

Representing Denmark Internationally, Questioned Belonging Nationally

Khalid was a 24-year-old young man whose family migrated to Denmark when he was only a few months old. Since arriving in Denmark, he and his family had lived in an inner-city neighbourhood in Copenhagen. Contrary to media representation of this neighbourhood, Khalid described growing up there as a positive experience. He grew up in an area that is popularly known for higher crime rates and social problems; however, the street he lived on was filled with good friends who shared his outlook on religiosity, ethical values, and academic ambition.

Although acknowledging the significance of his ethnic origin, Khalid emphasised his Danishness throughout his narrative. In fact, he took pride in having represented Denmark in international competitions as a national champion in a sport that he had practised since he was eight years old:

> I think the reason why I see myself as a Dane is the fact that I represented Denmark for eight years while on the national team. And when I

Middle-Class Muslim Respectability in Copenhagen 55

go out into the world and represent Denmark, then it's with the Danish flag and not the Moroccan or Turkish or something else. And people abroad also talk to you as if you're a Dane. We were in Vietnam for a tournament, I had to fight an Egyptian and it was just during the Cartoon Crisis. It was a couple of months after it happened and there was all that fuss, in 2005 or 2006. In my first fight, I faced Egypt, and they hated Denmark, the Arabs really hated Denmark. So, the guy I had to fight couldn't tell that I was Muslim. I just thought "How can you not see that?!" Then he looks at me and says: "I hate Denmark" before the fight, and I thought "Why would you say that before we fight?" then I just said: "*Assalamu 'alaikum akhi*" [Peace be with you, brother, translated from Arabic].

(Khalid, Copenhagen)

In this quote, Khalid describes representing Denmark in an international tournament during the Cartoon Crisis in 2006, when the country was now under massive global scrutiny. In this heated context—where the Danish media's negative representation of Muslims had received global attention—Khalid was in a position of having to represent Denmark in an international context that saw Denmark and its population as an anti-Muslim monolith. It surprised Khalid that his Egyptian opponent could not recognise the fact that Khalid himself was Muslim. Khalid responded by giving the Muslim greeting of peace, thereby challenging his "opponents" image of who Danes are.

Nevertheless, while Khalid represented Denmark internationally through his sports achievements, his Danishness was often questioned when competing nationally:

Something that's made me stay away from ethnic [i.e. white] Danes, I'm just going to say it: I have a lot of prejudice and those were already confirmed to me when I was really young, 9-10 years- old, a little cheeky kid, when we were out competing and had won gold, and we were waiting for our medals. It was in Esbjerg [a city in rural Jutland], when a man with a South- Jutland accent comes to me, you almost couldn't understand what he said. Then he says: "You're actually good at speaking Danish" [Khalid imitates a South-Jutland accent], then I said: "Sorry, what are you saying?", then he says: "Your Danish is good, a'right!". I just thought, of course I speak Danish, is there something wrong with you or what [laughs]. I told him: "I speak better Danish than you do". It wasn't just that experience, we've also been in Thisted, or whatever, Skanderborg, Århus, and all the other places. You're met with prejudice when you leave the environment you're used to here [in Copenhagen].

(Khalid, Copenhagen)

56   *Muslim Racialisation and its Affects*

His experiences internationally made it easy for Khalid to see himself as a Dane and be a representative of Denmark in the international sporting arena. However, admitting his own difficult relationship with white Danes, he also noted that whenever he had to travel and compete *within* Denmark (especially the rural parts of Denmark), he and his teammates – also Muslim and of ethnic minority background – would have to face the fact that they were often not perceived as Danes. The comment from the man from South Jutland in Khalid's quote was not intentionally racist. In fact, the man seemed to be complimenting Khalid on his Danish language skills. However, as a child, Khalid was made aware of his Danish non-belonging by the man's comments on his Danish skills. The man would not have made the same comment if Khalid had white-passing features.

Khalid explained that the challenge of feeling both Danish and Muslim had become less problematic as he ventured into professional life. Finishing his postgraduate degree before turning 25 and juggling several jobs in-between his studies, he engaged with Danish society as a professional and not a racialised youth from an inner-city neighbourhood defending his right to be perceived as Danish. Like Aisha, Iman, and Ahmad, once Khalid reached a certain level of social mobility through education, the power dynamics changed, and his ability to acquire respectability based on his class position enabled him to navigate the highly racialised terrain of Danish society. While these young "Muslims" influence on political, media, and policy discourses remain limited, their everyday interaction with white Danes challenges the public rhetoric and racialisation of young Muslims as "Others." Instead, the very definition of Danishness is what is being challenged, contested, negotiated, and redefined in these everyday interactions, where my interlocutors' adamant self-identification as simultaneously Danish and Muslim is fuelled by their social mobility.

Conclusion

This chapter explores how my interlocutors navigate the Danish terrain of racialisation. Whether in their everyday life or following media and political campaigns, the question of self-representation when experiencing the effects of racialisation filled a large part of young Muslims' narratives. Rytter and Pedersen (2014) look at the changes in Danish political and media rhetoric a decade after 9/11, and argue that immigrants and their descendants, particularly Muslims, have become highly visible in political and media discourses and, at the same time, increasingly silenced and excluded from engaging in these discourses (ibid., p. 2313). They argue that there has been a normalisation of Muslims as potentially dangerous in public discourse as well as in the way they are represented in securitisation and integration policies. They thus conclude that a "decade of suspicion" will inevitably affect Danish Muslims and their relationships with the majority population (Rytter & Pedersen, 2014, p. 2317).

Middle-Class Muslim Respectability in Copenhagen 57

Drawing on these perspectives, this chapter has presented cases of young Muslims who have been affected in various ways by the increased focus on immigrants and Muslims in public debates since 9/11. These young people's concern with responding to Muslim racialisation has become an important factor in their lives. In this context, their academic successes became important factors to establish their respectability and middle-class positioning. In turn, their social positioning enabled them to establish a strong counter-narrative to the idea of the hijab-wearing immigrant woman who does not speak "proper" Danish or the delinquent and potentially dangerous "non-Western" man who cannot stay out of trouble. Since most of my interlocutors were highly educated, they represented a minority among the Muslim population in Denmark. Thus, through their middle-class positioning, they had a greater capacity to defy their inferiorisation through performances of respectability. Nonetheless, they still struggled with having their Danishness and belonging questioned and undermined in everyday life.

It might seem that the young people represented in this chapter essentialise the individual white Dane to the political rhetoric of Islamophobic sentiments. However, it became clear to me—as my rapport with my participants grew—that this was one of the consequences of the othering-discourse that has penetrated the general public. In reality, these young Muslims engaged in and had meaningful relationships with white Danes that did not simply adopt the "us vs them" dichotomy. Rather, they had white friends, colleagues, and coaches that challenged the racist and Islamophobic rhetoric purported in political discourse. These relationships only became apparent to me when I stopped asking them about being Muslim in Denmark—a topic that is rigged with feelings of alienation and marginalisation from a "raceless" Danish society—and instead asked them to demonstrate what was important in their lives through city tours (see Chapter 4).

3 Gendered Islamophobia, Representation, and the Hijab in Montreal

In January 2017, the spotlight on Muslims in Quebec reached a tragic crescendo with a mass shooting in which French-Quebecer Alexandre Bissonette shot and killed six men and wounded 19 men attending the evening prayers in a mosque located in the capital city of Quebec (Mahrouse, 2018). In early fall 2017, less than a year after the mosque shooting, the Liberal government led by Philippe Couillard proposed and passed Bill 62: *An Act to foster adherence to State religious neutrality and, in particular, to provide a framework for requests for accommodations on religious grounds in certain bodies.* This bill would prohibit women wearing niqab from accessing public services. Two years later, in 2019, the Quebec government passed another bill, Bill 21, which prohibits public employees from wearing the hijab and other religious symbols. The Quebec mass shooting and the province's prohibition on Muslim and religious attire are rarely discussed in conjunction. They might even be seen as juxtaposing. One is an expression of lawlessness and inconceivable violence, and the other an expression of political cultural regulation to attain social coherence. However, Bissonette's illiberal racism and his violent annihilation of the Muslim Other cannot be disconnected from the liberal racism of the Quebec government in its mainstreaming of the threat of the Other. This is the main argument Mondon and Winter (2020) make regarding how liberal nation-states create environments that enable illiberal racist views to exist. Quebec's prohibition of Muslim signifiers such as the hijab can be read as invisibilising the Other, attempting to assimilate differences and maintain French supremacy.

The hijab and niqab have been a hotly debated topic in both Quebec and Denmark for many years. Both during my fieldwork and in the years that followed, there have been many attempts to prohibit both the hijab and the niqab in public spaces in both societies. Needless to say, both Quebec and Denmark (not to mention several other countries in the Global North), are particularly concerned with how Muslim women dress. In fact, one report by Open Society on restrictions on Muslim women's dress in EU member states and the United Kingdom demonstrates the various ways hijab or niqab-wearing women are discriminated against in everyday life. Such discrimination is not simply enacted through legal prohibitions but also in unofficial ways by

DOI: 10.4324/9781003294696-5

Gendered Islamophobia, Representation, and the Hijab in Montreal 59

restricting Muslim women's access to employment, sports activities, education, political participation, etc. (Open Society Justice Initiative, 2022).

There has been a lot of valuable academic scrutiny of the West's preoccupation with Muslim women's attire. Joan Scott's *Politics of the Veil* (2009) offers a historical analysis of France's colonial, racist, and political preoccupation with unveilling Muslim women. Likewise, Lila Abu Lughod's *Do Muslim Women Need Saving?* (2013) questions the West's attempt to "save" Muslim women from their cultures, emphasising how this narrative is disconnected from the realities of Muslim women's everyday lives. Building on these and other feminist scholarship, Sahar Ghumkor's more recent *The Political Psychology of the Veil* (2019) offers a Lacanian critical analysis of the West's obsession with Muslim women's veiled bodies. In this, she argues that the hijab/niqab and visible female Muslimness demonstrate the white liberal dream of freeing the Muslim woman through often corporal and punitive boundaries. In these critical feminist writings on the veil, the focus is on the racialised power dynamic of the West and its attempts to discipline the Muslim woman and her attire to hegemonic demands of white liberal ideals of femininity. Building on this line of work, this chapter shifts the focus away from the hegemonic Western paradigm on the hijab and instead emphasises Muslims' experiences of this paradigm.

My fieldwork in Montreal coincided with a political controversy on religious symbols triggered by the Quebec provincial government, the nationalist Parti Québécois (PQ). In 2013, the government proposed a new bill titled: *Charter affirming the values of State secularism and religious neutrality and of equality between women and men, and providing a framework for accommodation requests.* The bill was popularly known as the Charter of Values and was intended to ban all religious symbols in public institutions. Although presented as a general bill against all religious symbols, the media storm that ensued particularly focused on Muslim women wearing the hijab in Quebec, who would be greatly affected if the bill passed legislation. The Charter debate sets the stage for my Montreal-based fieldwork. This chapter will not focus on the hijab itself, but rather use the controversy to discuss how Quebec Muslims formulate, reproduce, and contest ideas of community (groupness) and representation through the hijab. The concept of a 'Muslim community' was an important frame of reference for the young people I met in Montreal, and it had specific implications in their lives and social relationships. I started my fieldwork as the Charter debate was gaining momentum, and this ushered in a range of different responses among these young Muslims. As I became more involved in their lives, the lack of uniformity in their responses, the difference in strategies, and even the disinterest of some made me question what they actually meant when they said they belonged to a "Muslim community."

By continuing to think with the concept of assemblage I introduced in the last chapter, the hijab is a clear signifier of Muslimness and thus an important part of the racialisation of Muslims, particularly Muslim women. The idea

60   *Muslim Racialisation and its Affects*

of the hijab is connected to a multitude of entities from state interests, power dynamics, gender relations to social identification, and community representation. The choice of wearing the hijab may be a personal dynamic process between spirituality and social life. However, most of the societal and political interest in the hijab disconnects it from its spiritual, dynamic, and processual character. It often reduces it to a social and sometimes political project of either oppression or emancipation. The ultimate consequence of this reductive approach is an objectification of the hijab as a signifier of Muslim oppression. The threat of governments prohibiting the hijab becomes a threat to Muslim agency and expression. Because of this threat, it becomes a way of re-producing the reification of the hijab as understood within Western paradigm. Within this space, there is little scope to explain the choice of hijab without using Western liberal discourse of emancipation and resistance. The consequence is often concealing any spiritual or alternative explanations that cannot be understood within a liberal paradigm.

By centering the perspectives and experiences of the young women I met during my fieldwork in Montreal, the chapter discusses the processes of groupness, i.e., creating a sense of Muslim community, through reified symbols such as the hijab. Thus, the hijab as a reified and contested symbol of female Muslimness becomes an entryway to discuss the wider idea of constructing the social group. I use Rogers Brubaker's (2004) conceptualisation of groupism to explore how "the group" is constructed and staged through events of resistance and mobilisation against government campaigns against supposedly ostentatious religious symbols. Through the detailed ethnographic material presented in the cases of this chapter, I argue for the importance of exploring the intricacies of belonging to a particular social group. How do individuals see themselves vis-à-vis others who share the same identification? What are the processes involved in constructing such groupness or "community feeling"?

Processes of Groupness and Community

As I ventured into the Montreal field during a heightened political drama and focus on Muslims in Quebec, I was faced with my own sense of frustration over the stereotypes being propagated in the media. My feelings were reciprocated by some of the young women I met, such as Layla, who I will introduce in more detail later. As part of my participant observation, I joined in a community protest organised by a young woman, Farida, who brought a larger group of young women together to bring awareness to the ongoing debate on the hijab. I accompanied Layla during this protest, where we were tasked with handing out flowers and a sympathetic letter explaining "our" perspective on wearing the hijab to passersby at a Montreal metro station. By this point in my fieldwork, I had participated in numerous protests, rallies, and community debates discussing the various sides of the Charter of Values debate. However, this was the first event I participated in where I felt

Gendered Islamophobia, Representation, and the Hijab in Montreal 61

uneasy with my participation. Reflexively, I knew this had something to do with my personal disagreement with the political approach this particular protest took. I felt apprehensive about attempting to appease the public with flowers and hijabs colour coordinated in Quebec's provincial flag. It was a drastically different approach than the critique that had dominated all the other protests I had attended. Nevertheless, I was well prepared with the unease that sometimes accompanies participant observation, because it is an immersive intersubjective experience that can sometimes challenge personal and political boundaries. I was, however, surprised to hear Layla share the same unease as myself. We both shared a similar logic of the unfairness of the propagated political stereotypes of Muslim women during the Charter debates. Furthermore, we were both more inclined to be unapologetic in our response, seeking political equality rather than the general public's sympathy. From the point of view of an outside observer, Layla, myself, and the rest of the young women involved in the event all seemed similar; dressed in a similarly coloured blue hijab with an attached white flower (representing the *fleurs-de-lis* of the Quebec provincial flag). No one would suspect the internal disagreements or different objectives of our participation. However, to paraphrase Layla's decision to participate, she would rather be supportive of the group's cause rather than refrain from helping based on her political opinion about fighting the Charter of Values as discriminatory. It is in this logic of participating for the sake of the group and representing a "united front" that the notion of groupness is established. In other words, groups do not exist until they are *performed* (Brubaker, 2004). And once the spectacle, event, or "community activity" is over, the group returns once again to being individuals who simply share a social category.

Most of the rallies, demonstrations, and debates I attended during the Charter debate represented a very diverse Montreal—not solely Muslims—coming together to construct a sense of community across social categories in solidarity with the targeted population groups. While Muslim women drew most of the public attention, other religious communities also felt targeted, such as turban-wearing Sikhs and kippah-wearing Jewish men. To analytically scrutinise the relationship between social category and social group, it became essential to understand how my participants relate to the idea of group and community (Brubaker, 2002, p. 169).

Anthropologists have historically tended to seek the group as the focal point of social study. However, we often risk a reified understanding of social groups that can potentially forfeit our understanding of the individual experience, agency, and capacity to act through, with, and sometimes in spite of the group. Nonetheless, the concept of group was inevitably implicated when researching young people in Montreal, who self-identify as Muslims. Their identifications, the stereotypes that surround them, and their process of belonging to a particular religious community are influenced by their notion of belonging to a "Muslim group." In this chapter, I explore this concept of group, not as an analytical concept, but as a concept *in the field*.

62   *Muslim Racialisation and its Affects*

In other words, as Brubaker argues, the concept of group cannot be taken for granted—it needs to be questioned. When and how is it relevant? And how is the idea of group implicated in people's lives and narratives? The concept of group is thus an emic concept and not an etic one. In Brubaker's words, it "is a key part of what we want to explain, not what we want to explain things *with*, it belongs to our empirical data, not our analytical toolkit" (2002, p. 165).

Brubaker uses the concept of groupism to define the tendency to take groups as "discrete, sharply differentiated, internally homogenous and externally bounded [...] as basic constituents of social life, chief protagonists of social conflicts, and fundamental units of social analysis" (2002, p. 164). Instead, he suggests using groupness as a concept to investigate groups. Groupness is the idea that groups are not an entity but are contextual and fluctuating; it is something that happens (ibid., p. 168). While Brubaker mainly focuses on groupness related to ethnicity, race, and nationalism, the concept is just as relevant in the context of understanding young Muslims' lives in a Western context. Their religious identification is often confounded with the notion of Muslims as a social entity "to which interests and agency can be attributed" (Brubaker, 2002, p. 162). In other words, as with ethnic, racial, and national categories, there is a tendency to reify and racialise Muslims as an internally homogenous and externally bounded group. This is what Garner and Selod (2015) refer to as the process of Muslim racialisation (see Introduction).

Such racialisation is often represented in political and media discourse on Muslims as a population group. However, as will become clear in this chapter, my interlocutors themselves often reified their Muslimness in monolithic terms, which in turn affected their sense of groupness. In fact, although I sought to explore individual experiences of being a young Muslim in Montreal, almost all of my interlocutors referred to the concept of "the Muslim community" as a social entity they were engaged in or related to. However, as with the concept of group, the idea of community needs to be analysed and contextualised. As Vered Amit suggests (2010), community is a concept that is good to think with. In this case, because it is so frequently used by the young Muslims I met, it becomes a concept *for* analysis rather than an analytical concept similar to the concept of groupness. When I refer to community in this chapter, I am thus referring to how my participants understand the concept, which is often a localised, highly specific group of people who share religious, educational, and social ties (e.g. the Muslim Student Association [MSA] at Montreal's universities).

Quebec Nationalism and (Un)reasonable Accommodation

Within the Quebec context, it is controversial to speak of racism in conjunction with nationalism. The separatist nationalist movement in Quebec was founded on the resistance of the cultural and economic domination of English Canada. In the 1960s, during the Quiet Revolution and the rise of the

Gendered Islamophobia, Representation, and the Hijab in Montreal 63

separatist movement, prominent French Quebeckers went as far as comparing their subordination to English Canada with the oppression experienced by African Americans. David Austin argues that Quebec's positioning as a minority vis-à-vis Canada neglected its own racist treatment of both indigenous, Black, and immigrant populations (Austin, 2010). This culminated in the loss of the 1995 Quebec referendum to gain sovereignty from federal Canada. At the time, the Quebec-separatist premier Jacques Parizeau infamously said: "It's true that we have been beaten, but basically by what? By money and the ethnic vote, essentially" (Jacques Parizeau, Quebec Referendum, 1995). With these comments, Parizeau influenced the Quebec independence movement from its progressive roots of combating the marginalisation of French Quebeckers towards a more explicitly right-leaning political rhetoric focusing on French nationalism and supremacy. Throughout the following decade, different controversies related to immigrants and religious communities ensued. Within this context, the debate on hijab as well as niqab has been ongoing since 1995, when the Quebec Human Rights Commission ruled that it should be permissible for girls to wear the hijab. Nevertheless, the controversy surrounding hijab and niqab in public space continues to reappear in political and media discourse. Similarly, controversies over other religious accommodations arose. In 2007, a media controversy broke out concerning the religious accommodation of a Muslim group visiting a *cabane à sucre*[1] (sugar shack). Visitors objected to the group being served meals without pork, which is traditionally served, as well as the small group praying in the waiting room near the reception hall (Fossum, 2009, p. 86). There have also been controversies surrounding reasonable accommodations for other religious minorities. For instance, in 2001, there was a case against a Sikh student in a Montreal school who was not allowed to wear his *kirpan* (a blunt ceremonial dagger part of the religious dress Sikh men wear) to school. He took the case to the Canadian Supreme Court, who ruled he should have been permitted to wear the *kirpan* to school (Maillé & Salée, 2013). In 2006, a controversy arose concerning a YMCA gym in Montreal that was located near a Jewish school. School administrators complained that their students could view women dressed in athletic attire exercising in front of a large gym window and consequently paid the gym to frost the window. Women attending the gym complained about the accommodation, and as with the case about the Muslim group visiting the sugar shack and the Sikh student wearing a *kirpan*, a moral panic arose in news media questioning whether reasonable accommodations had gone too far (Fossum, 2009, p. 86). In response to the media representations of these cases, the leader of the then Action Démocratique du Québec (ADQ), a right-wing, conservative political party,

---

1 Small cabins where maple syrup is produced; certain times during the year, these cabins open up their reception hall and serve meals made with maple syrup as well as different outdoor activities to the public.

64 Muslim Racialisation and its Affects

Mario Dumont claimed the level of accommodations that were being granted religious communities was absurd and contradicted Quebec values (ibid).

These racialising controversies about "the migrant threat" led the then Liberal government to create the *Consultation Commission on Accommodation Practices Related to Cultural Differences* headed by Professors Gérard Bouchard and Charles Taylor (Bouchard & Taylor, 2008). They were to investigate the accommodation practices of cultural differences, consult individuals and organisations on their opinions, and finally give their recommendations based on their findings (Bouchar & Taylor, 2008, p. 15). The Bouchard/Taylor commission's recommendations can be summarised into five main categories: (1) defining policies related to interculturalism and secularism; (2) improving integration policies; (3) improving intercultural practices in public institutions; (4) ensuring adequate training for and accountability of institutions dealing with citizens; and (5) addressing the under-representation of ethnic minorities in public services, combating discrimination, offering support to immigrant women, and ensuring economic and social rights in the Québec Charter (Bouchard & Taylor, 2008). The commission defined Québec interculturalism as an alternative to federal Canada's approach to multiculturalism by emphasising the position of the French language. In this way, interculturalism is understood as "the acceptance of and communication and interaction between culturally diverse groups, without, however, implying any intrinsic equality among them" (Anctil, 2011, p. 23). Hence, diversity is encouraged, however only under the condition that the "supremacy of French in the language and culture of Québec" is acknowledged (ibid.).

Although the Bouchard/Taylor report, published in 2008, downplayed the issues of Québec's racism, in 2010 the debate resurfaced with the proposed Bill 94 titled: *An Act to establish guidelines governing accommodation requests within Administration and certain institutions.* The bill, which was later scrapped, sought to prohibit women wearing niqab—the face veil—from working in public institutions or using public services. Bill 94 was the predecessor to the Charter of Values (also known as Bill 60), which the government sought to implement in the fall of 2013, followed by a niqab-prohibition in 2018 and a 2019-prohibition for public employees to wear the hijab (and other religious symbols).

This reoccurring debate on reasonable accommodations revolves around religious minority practices deemed as non-Quebecker. Looking at the reasonable accommodation debate from a historical perspective, Pierre Anctil provides an overview of Quebeckers' reaction to the growing ethnic, cultural, and religious diversity in their society (2011). To fully appreciate this reaction, Québec history needs to be understood in the context of the French resistance to British rule before the 20th century, which gave rise to nationalist movements, analogous to the Irish and Scottish movements in other places of colonial Britain. Fast-forwarding to 1971, the then federal government led by Prime Minister Pierre Trudeau proposed an official language policy

Gendered Islamophobia, Representation, and the Hijab in Montreal   65

along with multiculturalism. This meant that French and English languages were recognised as the official languages of the country, which were incumbent on immigrants to learn without requiring the adoption of either the French or English cultures. However, based on the Bouchard/Taylor commission's recommendations, Québec formed its own response to the notion of multiculturalism: interculturalism. Canadian multiculturalism promotes the equal rights of the cultural and ethnic minorities within a society, at least in legal policies. Quebec interculturalism, however, limits cultural and linguistic diversity. Here, cultural and linguistic expressions need to be situated within a hierarchical structure with the supremacy of French language and culture (Anctil, 2011). The controversy surrounding whether immigrants need reasonable accommodation is placed within a broader discourse of immigrants threatening French language and culture (Bakali, 2015). Hence, Freiwald highlights that "the conflict that haunts interculturalism in Québec is rather between two rival models of community: nation (premised on peoplehood) and citizenship" (Freiwald, 2011, p. 85). Ultimately, the political discourse may acknowledge the fact that immigrants can become legal citizens; however, they may still be excluded from the Québec nation based on their lack of conformity with white French Québec culture.

This historical background is important in order to understand the Parti Québécois (PQ) government's attempt to limit religious symbols in public spaces in 2013. Coincidentally, the Charter of Values was introduced by Parti Québécois Minister Bernard Drainville around the time I began my fieldwork in Montreal. The Charter sought to prohibit certain forms of religious dress in public institutions—in the name of *laïcité* (secularity)—following similar bans in France. In the nine months in which I conducted fieldwork in Montreal, I observed and participated in events addressing the Charter debate until its culmination in the PQ government's political defeat to the Liberals in the elections of April 2014. During the Charter debates, however, the PQ deployed an extensive PR campaign promoting the bill in provincial media and public space (e.g., posters in metro-stations, news segments on TV, and public/local debates), resulting in province-wide discussions and public hearings. The debate consisted mostly of two opposing views: citizens challenging the bill as an infraction on personal freedoms versus citizens supporting the bill as an important expression of Québec's secularity and gender equality. PQ politicians led by Pauline Marois and Bernard Drainville constructed a political crisis that focused on identity politics underlining the exclusionary nature of Québec identity. Ultimately, by attempting to strengthen a sense of ethnic cohesion among *Québécois de souche* (white French Quebecers), the PQ government targeted ethnic and religious communities to highlight their otherness and need to conform to "essential" Quebec values such as *laïcité*. As an easy target (possibly because of their more recent migration history or visibility in dress and ethnicity), Muslims, and Muslim women in particular, took the brunt of the attention during the Charter debate.

66   Muslim Racialisation and its Affects

This rather detailed background on Québec's national(ist) history and controversies related to immigrants and religious communities is important to recognise how Muslims are positioned vis-à-vis Québec nationalism. All of the young Montrealers I met spoke both English and French, although some were better at one or the other language. The fact that they were either bilingual or trilingual (most also spoke their parents' mother tongue) meant that their national identification was not limited to Québec but included federal Canada. One young man, Isam, who moved to Montreal from Morocco when he was 1 year old, described this identification very succinctly:

> I definitely see myself as a Canadian as well, I see Montreal as my city, not so much Québec [the province], although I love the French language. But I don't associate it with the Québec province. I think it's because of the whole separatist issue. It's just a matter of loyalty. Canada was the country that gave me citizenship, and I don't agree with the whole separatist thing. I never felt that Canada oppressed me because of my language [French]. I do understand that happened but I don't feel it's my battle. I grew up being accepted for the language I speak [French].
>
> (Isam, Montreal)

Young Muslims' ability to connect with Canada as a national identity in the face of racist discourse and policies meant that during a controversy such as the Charter debate, several young people were seriously considering a move out of Québec. This rhetoric of identifying with federal Canada (despite French being their first language) was a unique possibility that the youth in Denmark did not have.

Becoming a Representation of "Islam"

Layla was a 25-year-old international student attending one of Montreal's French universities. I knew her prior to beginning my fieldwork in 2013, so when I invited her to participate, she was eager to help. On a cold November afternoon, we met at her university campus after she finished her classes. Before our interview, however, we both needed to pray the afternoon prayer. Upon completing *wudo* [ablution], Layla took me to the prayer spot that she and other Muslim students had unofficially adopted as their own. The prayer corner was in the building basement, next to student lockers, where people rarely passed by. It was my first time visiting this campus, and I was surprised at the difference in prayer facilities between the English and French universities. Layla shrugged and explained that it had been a long and ongoing battle to try to acquire an office space for the Muslim Student Association, not to mention a prayer space. We prayed and found an abandoned classroom in which to conduct the interview. We sat down to talk, and given our prior acquaintance, the interview discussion proceeded informally with little direction on my part.

Gendered Islamophobia, Representation, and the Hijab in Montreal 67

As an international student from Morocco, Layla explained her move to Montreal in very transformative terms. She was only 19 years old when her parents sent her off to start university in Montreal. Though her brother would join her 6 months later, Layla's need to establish herself alone in a new city was an overwhelming experience. To ease the transition, she resorted to what was familiar to her: choreographed dance. In Morocco, she had lived a very active lifestyle and had been competing in hip-hop dance since she was 12 years old. So, in search of familiarity, Layla looked up a local dance studio she could join. She formed her first friendships there and, as she put it, "came in direct contact with Canadians." She struggled, however, to keep up with the dance group's ambitions while also sorting out her immigration papers and starting university. Following a snowboarding accident that prevented her from dancing, she drifted away from the dance group. She explained that while settling down in Montreal, forging new friendships and getting to know a new city, she felt "all over the place," unable to commit to any extracurricular activities Simultaneously, she described searching for a deeper spiritual meaning that could help ease her transition, which she found in Islam. She felt torn:

> The choice was between religion and the Canadian way of life, because I was always half [invested in each]. [Only partly in] the [dance] group because I'm not drinking alcohol, I'm not going to the club, I don't have a boyfriend, I'm doing Ramadan. All those things make me foreign.[2]
>
> (Leyla, Montreal)

In this quote, Layla indicates the struggle she felt trying to be a part of her dance group and "the Canadian way of life" it represented, and at the same time maintaining her religious values. With this challenge to find her place in her new society, the question of how Layla represented herself to the world around her became significant. She struggled with the fact that because she did not wear a hijab, her non-Muslim friends did not recognise the extent of her religious commitment. She explained how they assumed she was "just like anyone else" until they learnt that she prayed and celebrated Ramadan. Only then did they notice she was "different," as she put it. Layla was uncomfortable with this lack of initial recognition. She described a feeling of guilt over the way in which she appeared to the world:

> [...W]hen you're with non-Muslims, you're always compared to "Oh, what are you doing?", and you feel like you cannot give them the

---

2 Layla's quotes are included *ad verbatim* with minimal corrections. It is important to mention that Layla was very articulate in French and spoke it with great fluency; however, because of my limited French skills, she agreed to conduct the interview in English. This confidence demonstrates her ability and willingness to engage with both language communities in Montreal.

answer, and you are not representing how [Islam] has to be. So maybe I was a good person, but I was not a good Muslim. I was doing the half. So, I'm not feeling Muslim, because I'm just doing like a half-Muslim.

(Leyla, Montreal)

The issues Layla described do not necessarily concern how others perceived her. Rather, it was more about how she saw herself through her interaction with particular people. This is where the question of representation becomes pertinent. Layla was uncomfortable with the type of Muslim she thought that the world (read: her Montreal social spaces) saw in her; she did not feel it properly represented "Islam".

There are several interesting factors that appear in Layla's narrative regarding her initial settlement in Montreal. Coming from an affluent family and growing up in a large Moroccan city, life in the urban metropolis of Montreal was not foreign to her. In fact, she easily reconnected with her well-known hobbies and lifestyle, which gave her an avenue to develop relationships outside the typical international student environment that many international students often turn to. In Morocco, the question of representing "Islam" was never an issue. Everyone around her was Muslim and she simply lived her religiosity without giving it a second thought. However, in Montreal, Layla was suddenly asked about her religious beliefs, and why other Muslim women wore hijab, and she did not. From never being questioned on her Muslimness to it suddenly becoming a central focus of her encounters with non-Muslims, she started to feel a heavy burden to represent her religiosity in the "right" way. Thus, once she decided 2 years later to wear the hijab, she finally felt ready to represent the Muslim role she felt was expected of her:

I don't want to wear hijab and just be in my bubble with my Muslim hijabi girls. It's not a good thing because when I wear hijab I want to show non-Muslims what is hijab and to interact with them and to have one hijabi in their life to say: "She's normal".

(Leyla, Montreal)

Now that Layla felt she was able to "represent Islam," she did not shy away from her Muslimness and actively opposed Muslim stereotypes. Through personal relationships, she ensured that at least her friends did not believe the Islamophobic stereotypes that were often attributed to hijab-wearing women. In facing racialising political discourse, which essentialises individuals into broad monolithic categories of "the Muslim Other," Layla, and several other young women, responded by trying to represent the quintessential Muslim within their surroundings. However, in doing so, they often risked reducing their nuanced lives, experiences, and opinions into yet another monolithic representation of Muslims as a homogenous group. Throughout Layla's narrative, it is apparent that her personal friendships with non-Muslims and

Gendered Islamophobia, Representation, and the Hijab in Montreal 69

engagements in social issues, such as helping people with disabilities, go beyond her own representational narrative. However, her narrative highlights how racialisation processes through dominant political and popular discourse affect young Muslims' identification. Such discourse creates a feeling of needing to construct counter-narratives that challenge the image of Muslim female inferiority. This came into play in Layla's life, whenever she encountered prejudice because of her hijab:

> You feel like you have more to show, two times, that you are capable to do it. Because the normal – what people do – is not enough, you have to show more and more that "I'm normal, I have the competence". That makes you tired, to try and try and try to prove something you've already proven but no, it's not enough, you have to prove it more.
>
> (Leyla, Montreal)

Leyla resists the racialisation of Muslim women as passive and submissive. Yet, to do so, she must work harder and gain less credit for her efforts. The image of the oppressed Muslim woman has been proliferated by Quebec politicians through the Charter debates and other similar campaigns and trickled down to everyday encounters, affecting Leyla's ability to contest these images. Nevertheless, her own response to this was a more relaxed attitude:

> Personally, I try to not internalize that image, the fact that I know this is your perception of me, helps me not to victimize myself. That's why it doesn't bother me what they think. [...]. That's why it doesn't touch me, because that's not the definition I choose.
>
> (Leyla, Montreal)

Layla contended that being conscious of existing stereotypes enables one to oppose them. She took a critical stance towards self-victimisation in the face of discrimination and Islamophobia. Nevertheless, she could not escape the fact that because of the prevalent perception of Muslim women as subordinate, she was still forced to prove herself—on behalf of *all* Muslim women—when someone vocalised their Islamophobic opinion about what she supposedly represented.

Public Representation as Self-identification

Fadila was a 19-year-old young woman. She was born in France, lived the first 6 years of her life in Morocco before her family finally settled in Montreal. As she described it, her parents hated life in Morocco, and France was not much better, but they loved Montreal. Here, it seemed, they were staying for good. Her parents were active in local Muslim organisations and felt settled in the city. Fadila developed her sense of Canadian belonging based on her parents' attachment to Montreal. As she explained it, she

70 *Muslim Racialisation and its Affects*

may have had a Moroccan background, but she identified herself as a North American. I first met Fadila during the Blue Hijab event, which she almost single-handedly organised. I later met her again at an English university in Montreal, where she had just begun attending her undergraduate studies. In our conversations, she described in detail how her activism had developed. Although she had attended a Muslim primary school in Montreal, she was one of the few Muslim students in her high school and CEGEP.[3] She wore the hijab, Fadila explained, but also accommodated her style of dress to the mainstream standards of her classmates:

> Right now, I feel I'm wearing the most modest thing I can wear but before I was wearing skinny jeans, I was wearing tight stuff, and why? Because I felt like I wasn't accepted or something, but it's really something internal, it has nothing to do with what people were thinking, it was really what I was thinking they were thinking about me. So, it's something that really influenced what I was thinking. Especially when you're 15–16.
>
> (Fadila, Montreal)

At the age of 16 years, Fadila was struggling to fit in among her peers, and therefore adapted her attire to feel less conspicuous among them while still wearing the hijab.

Fadila started at an English university, where she found a great deal of cultural diversity. Her hijab was less noticeable here, and she therefore felt more comfortable with appearing different. With investing less attention on how she appeared to her surroundings, she dedicated herself more actively to social issues she cared about. Fadila explained that because of her parents' activism in a local Muslim community centre, she was brought up to appreciate the importance of engaging with societal issues. This experience gave her the motivation to get involved in issues she felt strongly about:

> In that summer, the things that were happening in Egypt and Syria, and I started going out and demonstrating. I actually went to Ottawa to support the people of Rabi'a [Egyptian protest movement]. And Syria. I started helping with people outside [the Muslim community center]. And then while I was at [university], I decided to fill my time to help others.
>
> Because at some point I realized that my time is precious, and I have to use it wisely. I got involved with Amnesty International in September. I was doing stuff with [a friend], and then I started [an organization].

---

3 CEGEP is a French acronym for "*Collège d'enseignement général et professionnel*" [General and Vocational College], which is a pre-university college that is part of Quebec's education system.

Gendered Islamophobia, Representation, and the Hijab in Montreal 71

Did you hear about it? It was basically all going on with the Charter. So, with the Charter, I went out demonstrating against the Charter. And beginning this project took a lot of my time.

(Fadila, Montreal)

Fadila was volunteering in several projects; however, when the controversy surrounding the Charter began, an elder at the local Muslim community centre urged Fadila to get involved. It was Fadila's responsibility, he argued, to defend hijab-wearing women from the Charter. Fadila felt compelled to spearhead a project that would voice her concerns about the Charter, and this resulted in the Blue Hijab event. She worked on this event almost full time for three months. At the time of our interview, this event—having been implemented successfully—was still very important to her. The drama of the Charter was still ongoing, and she wanted to broaden the initial scope of the organisation from its focus on the Charter to an organisation that educated others about cultural differences. She explained:

So, when I take a position in this project, I don't talk about politics, I don't talk about economics, I concentrate only on the social issues. So, there's a work, education you have to do on people, and education is not like, you can't do just an event like this [the Blue Hijab event]. Even if you plan it very well, you can't just do 4 hours of staying in a town and talking about education because education is a constant process. You have to work on it and work on it. So, I'm still planning a trip, we're going to Quebec [city] this time, and it's not going to be only Muslim people, not only women, it's going to be all kinds of people, who will go to Quebec. Whatever their background, whether they are atheist, religion, no religion, people who feel like we should concentrate on values that unify us instead of dividing us.

(Fadila, Montreal)

Fadila took her role to "educate" people about the negative stereotyping of Muslims very seriously. The question of representation to Fadila was more public than personal as opposed to Layla's case, who wanted to develop personal friendships to counter political and media racialisation of Muslims. For Fadila, it was her public and social responsibility to ensure that a broader public changed their perception of Muslims, and that meant organising public events in which she and her friends from the community centre would represent a different image of Muslims.

Evoking the Group: Flattening Differences

Layla and Fadila had different life histories and experiences that brought them to different ways of engaging with the Muslim community vis-à-vis white hegemonic structures. Layla was politically savvy, perhaps even jaded.

72 Muslim Racialisation and its Affects

She saw no point in attempting to disprove the Islamophobic assumption of her inferiority. She understood the power element at play. Racism and Islamophobia would persist even if all her non-Muslim friends understood and accepted her Muslim lifestyle. Thus, Layla's strategy was more about her interpersonal skills to form friendships with people of diverse backgrounds and through that challenge the effects of powerful racialisation processes. Six years younger than Layla, Fadila was more politically hopeful, maybe even a bit naïve. She felt the burden of her social responsibility and believed she had to *do* something about countering Islamophobia on a large scale. However, to Fadila, racism and Islamophobia were not about power dynamics but rather general ignorance of what Islam "really is." She focused more on public counter-representation as performances of acceptability; hence, the Blue Hijab event adorned in Quebec's provincial colours and with flowers and chocolates to passersby. It is in this approach that the process of groupness becomes an apparent *strategy* for analysis. As Brubaker argues, "[b]y *invoking* groups, they seek to *evoke* them, summon them, call them into being. Their categories are *for doing*—designed to stir, summon, justify, mobilize, kindle and energize" (2002, p. 166). Fadila sought to bring people together to challenge the Islamophobic images about Muslim women. She took an apolitical stance by focusing on acceptability. Yet the subject of the hijab was already politicised through the Quebec governments' attempt to prohibit it. So, the field both Fadila and Leyla had to navigate had already politicised the hijab. In turn, as hijab-wearing women, they had also been politicised and thus their capacity to act was limited by the political terrain. So, how were they supposed to mobilise and challenge the racialisation of the hijab within a social field that had already reified their hijab to a political symbol of Otherness?

Layla and Fadila had different answers to this question. Their differing tactics posed different opportunities and limitations when challenging racist stereotypes. It is fascinating then to see what happens when Layla and Fadila, who share a similar identification (Muslim), disagree on how to contest the Charter. As mentioned previously, Layla—though she volunteered at Fadila's Blue Hijab event—had her reservations about the more appeasing apolitical approach of contesting the Charter and its accompanying polemics. For Layla, opposing the Charter was not a question of representing a different image of the Muslim woman than the one constructed by the Quebec government's Charter of Values campaign. Rather, it was a political issue of discrimination, and needed to be addressed as such. In contrast, Fadila— wanting to avoid the question of politics—wrote a letter distributed publicly during the Blue Hijab event that sought to appeal to readers' sympathies. Layla carefully voiced her concerns to the organisers regarding the event's lack of political resistance towards what she perceived as racist politics. These concerns were, however, overlooked as the event had already been planned out. She thus acquiesced and volunteered for the sake of solidarity with the organisers.

Gendered Islamophobia, Representation, and the Hijab in Montreal 73

It is interesting to note here how careful Layla was not to offend the team of organisers, although she disagreed with their approach. Given her attention to the prevalent discourse on Muslim women as submissive and oppressed, she felt uncomfortable with the letter being distributed during the Blue Hijab event, which she found to be apologetic and too appeasing. Nevertheless, to present a united front, Layla chose to support Fadila's initiative, thus depicting a coherent resistance movement of Muslim women. It is through such flattening of disagreements and disputes that groups are invoked, as Brubaker describes it. This is done at the risk of reinforcing the reification of "the group" as a stable homogenous monolith. Nevertheless, it did in fact enable these young women to mobilise against powerful political forces. To return to Saba Mahmood's point about agency as dependent on the political context, young Muslim women in Montreal could not escape the political; their agency, i.e. capacity to act, was contingent on the dominant political campaign of the hijab as opposing gender equality.

The campaigning against the Charter was just one example of many disagreements that happened among the young Montrealers on a regular basis related to community events, volunteering projects, and other social gatherings. The choice of consciously erasing disputes demonstrates an important aspect of groupness. Even with the risk of reifying the group and enforcing racialisation processes that represent Muslims as a monolith, the group must *appear* to share a united front and present itself as homogeneous, at least in the extraordinary events of mobilisation.

Conclusion

This chapter has explored the processes of groupness by examining gendered expressions of Muslimness through the hijab and the resistance of hijab prohibition in Quebec. I use the event of the Quebec Charter of Values controversy and the reification of the hijab to critique approaching the concept of social groups and community as *a priori* analytical concepts rather than empirical phenomena that are dynamic and fluid (Amit, 2002, 2010; Brubaker, 2004).

As I started my fieldwork in Montreal, participants kept talking about "the Muslim community" as an important aspect of their social framework and reason for getting involved in different events. I realised that their preoccupation with "the community" and "the Muslim group" was important, so I therefore needed to approach them as concepts that were good to think with (Amit, 2010). They were objects of analysis rather than analytical concepts (Brubaker, 2004). This chapter demonstrates how analysing processes of constructing groups and communities can be invaluable in depicting the nuances, complexity, and diversity among people who share a social identification. When we refrain from imposing our analytical concepts on our field, our interlocutors are empowered to share their own conceptualisation of these concepts. In turn, these emic concepts depict a negotiated and

74 *Muslim Racialisation and its Affects*

processual understanding of groupness, i.e. the construction of "the group" through social processes.

The young Muslims' concern with the "Muslim community" was unique to the Montreal setting. My Danish participants did not mention the concept of community in similar terms. However, "the community" that Montrealers referred to was not an abstract imagined community (Anderson, 2006). It was rather locally constructed through performances that brought together young people who shared the same social, economic, and cultural/religious backgrounds as themselves. In this way, they did not necessarily feel a sense of community with Muslims in a North African village, but rather felt a more localised and intersubjective sense of groupness with other young Montreal Muslims in higher education. It is this groupness that is continuously recreated through social and religious events *and* through public representations (e.g. the hijab or beard) to maintain a sense of "group" belonging.

Part II

Muslim Pathways and Spatial Narratives

4 Contesting Racialised Spaces in Copenhagen

In Chapter 2, I provide an analysis of how racialisation and class intersect in Denmark with a focus on young middle-class Muslims' experiences coming of age in post-9/11 Denmark. In this chapter, I want to take this analysis one step further to focus on the interconnected processes of racialisation and spatialisation. This chapter builds on the idea that racialisation is a process that is reproduced and experienced in social *and* spatial terms. In other words, since space is constituted through the social, it can therefore also be racialised. Case in point, Figure 4.1 is a city map of Copenhagen with a filter depicting where "non-Western" residents reside in the city in 2015. What is important to note here is that this map is not about the cultural diversity or ethnic make-up of the city. If it was, "non-Western" would be a "colour-blind" term that seeks to obscure the cultural, linguistic, and social diversity of citizens from the global majority. Rather, this interactive spatial map, developed by the Copenhagen municipality based on their own data as well as data from Statistics Denmark, focuses on "socioeconomic factors."[1] The map has other filters besides "non-Western" to measure levels of socioeconomic disparity in different Copenhagen neighbourhoods, including unemployment rates, low-income levels, and "feelings of safety." These factors become part of the racialisation of Copenhagen's spaces by adding "non-Western" as one of the markers to measure "socioeconomic" levels. The racial ascription becomes a way of differentiating between "white (affluent) space" (marked in light grey) and "non-Western (deprived) space" (marked in dark grey). Thus, a class-based spatial analysis of Copenhagen becomes intertwined with an analysis of the racialisation of spaces (Figure 4.1).

For me, growing up in Greater Copenhagen, this image of inner-city Copenhagen is a visualisation of how I socially navigated these spaces. I can read this map and the racialised and classed insinuations it portrays with ease. The map depicts which areas I can walk around "unmarked," and which areas I am hypervisible as a Muslim Other (Ahmed, 2000). Nonetheless, as a native to Copenhagen, I do not move so (self-)consciously through these spaces. In similar ways, the young Muslims I met navigated this (racialised) "socioeconomic" map

---

1 Copenhagen Municipality. (2015). Socioøkonomisk kort [Socioeconomic Map]. https://kbhkort.kk.dk/spatialmap?profile=sociokort

DOI: 10.4324/9781003294696-7

78 Muslim Pathways and Spatial Narratives

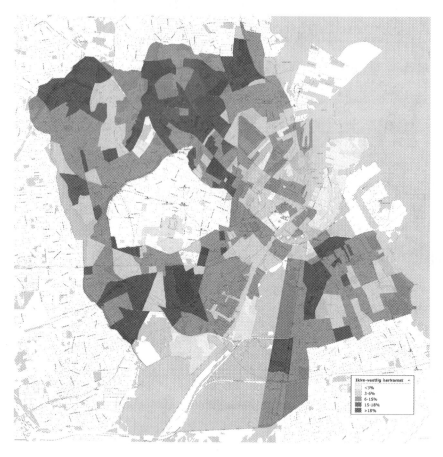

Figure 4.1 A screenshot of an interactive "socioeconomic" map over Copenhagen with a fiilter to show the percentage of residents of "non-Western heritage." Image reprinted with permission from Copenhagen municipality.

in their everyday life without much self-consciousness. They may have lived in the darker parts of the map, yet studied, worked, and socialised in the lighter parts or vice versa. Either way, they moved seamlessly through these spaces; rooted in some, while "invading" others (cf. (Puwar, 2004). It is this ease I want to emphasise in this chapter. As they formulated their spatial narratives through their city walks, they became conscious about navigating this map based on the social meaning attributed to particular neighbourhoods. They traversed the urban terrain according to the spatial narrative they *wanted* to tell me. Their comprehensive knowledge of the spatialisation of socioeconomic position of different spaces meant that they could implicitly critique the racialisation of "non-Western" socioeconomic inferiority as well as position themselves within the affluent white spaces in which their very presence is hypervisible.

Space as Text

Building on Caroline Knowles' idea of viewing space as text (Knowles, 2000), this chapter analyses how social actors inscribe meaning into space by intentionally navigating and manipulating the social connotations attached to particular spaces. Based on the spatial narratives of young Muslims in Copenhagen, this chapter looks at how movement through city spaces can become avenues to construct and represent social mobility. The spatial narratives in this chapter demonstrate different experiences of social mobility, yet similar notions of space as representative of current and prospective social positions.

The young Muslims I met would often narrate reasons why it was important to include one part of a high street while a different part of the same street was the exact opposite of what they wished to affiliate themselves with. By claiming some spaces and rejecting others, they demonstrated the selectiveness of a spatial narrative. The spaces my interlocutors *chose* to take me to became ways of constructing a particular subjectivity as demonstrated through city spaces.

The spatial tours I highlight in this chapter all included an exploration of Nørrebro, an inner-city area of Copenhagen that has a history of being a multicultural working-class neighbourhood (Schmidt, 2011). It has previously struggled with poverty and high crime rates, but parts of Nørrebro have experienced a level of gentrification in recent years, attracting a trendsetting, artistically orientated, and often white professional population, many of whom have immigrated from rural parts of Denmark. It even won "The World's Coolest Neighbourhood" by the *Time Out* magazine in 2021 (Time Out, 2021). Nørrebro can be compared to Williamsburg in Brooklyn, New York, or Brick Lane in East London—although on a much smaller scale. Similar to these global trendsetting neighbourhoods, Nørrebro has a working-class history but is quickly becoming one of the most popular areas to live for young people studying or working in Copenhagen. Nevertheless, at the point of my fieldwork in 2014, not all of Nørrebro had been gentrified, and my interlocutors were quick to inform me about which parts of it they identified with positively and which were the less attractive areas.

Besides Nørrebro, many interlocutors chose to show me different parts of downtown Copenhagen, including their favourite cafes and walking streets. In this sense, the narratives presented in this chapter demonstrate how spaces can be representations of social position rather than personal history. The three interlocutors whose tours I describe in this chapter do not know each other; yet, they all chose to focus their tours in particular areas of Copenhagen. I was surprised to discover that they wanted to take me to some of the same places and share with me the same notions of why some places are better than others. There seemed to be some sort of "common local knowledge" that Nørrebro north of the famous yellow wall of *Assistentens Cemetery* is a less charming place to

80 *Muslim Pathways and Spatial Narratives*

Figure 4.2 The yellow wall of the famous Assistentens Cemetery, where historical figures such as Søren Kierkegaard and HC Andersen are buried. Photograph taken by author.

associate with, or that some streets, cafes, and independent clothing stores were trendier than others (Figure 4.2). Much of this common knowledge depicts a similar "socioeconomic" map presented above. From among several tours I conducted in Copenhagen, I selected these three cases because they demonstrated different experiences of social and spatial mobility, and yet similar notions of space as representative of their current and prospective social positions.

Representing Social Mobility, Challenging Hegemonic Structures

When I gave my Danish participants the task of showing me their city, their emphasis was often on self-representation through city spaces. They displayed their social mobility by effortlessly moving through the yellow spaces on the map and highlighting the red spaces when relevant to their counter-narratives to racialised and "working-class" spaces as supportive and comforting environments as opposed to the initial discomfort of navigating through White space. I use the idea of White space, building on the ethnographic scholarship of Elijah Anderson (2022). In his book *Black in White Space,* Anderson conceptualises this idea by demonstrating how Black Americans and other

Contesting Racialised Spaces in Copenhagen 81

racialised people cannot avoid White space but rather must learn to navigate through these spaces. Among Danish Muslims, this was especially true when trying to cement their middle-class position in society. They put questions of social class and position at the forefront of their city tours with little direction from me. Through this counter-narrative, they emphasised their level of social mobility as a challenge to the existing stereotype of Muslim immigrants and descendants as an inferior social class.

Being young Copenhageners, my participants knew how to move through their city spaces. They lived in the surrounding suburbs of Copenhagen, often in common housing in the darker segments of the map.[2] However, when it came to depicting their city spaces, they all made conscious choices in what they wanted to show me to demonstrate their city life. They would show me the trendy café in the gentrified part of Nørrebro rather than the cheap shawarma shop in the less regenerated part of the district. It was a way of challenging the image of Muslims' socioeconomic inferiority by exploiting the narrative potential in rooting themselves in particular city spaces, which represented alternative images of "the Danish Muslim."

The young people I met were thus tactical in their choice of movements through the city, demonstrating their deep knowledge of the social connotations linked to particular spaces and areas. The cases I present in this chapter show how spatial accounts can be avenues to understand the everyday agency that social actors have regarding the city structures they move through. Spatial narratives become important representational accounts of these youth's subjectivity and their social mobility. These young Muslims may not have had the capacity to change the hegemonic meaning of particular spaces as socially deprived and racially inferior. These meanings have been etched into the map presented above and are used as important political and bureaucratic context to regulate and plan the urban space and particularly the racialised Others who live in parts of the city (Regeringen, 2018). Nevertheless, the youth could move past these spaces, they could disassociate from them, or perhaps even include them by re-narrating their significance as convivial inclusive spaces (Hassani, 2023b). Conviviality is a concept introduced by Paul Gilroy (2004): he defines it as the interaction, cohabitation, communal engagements across racialised, ethnic, cultural, religious, and social differences in everyday life. Such engagements exist despite the structural racism and inequality of wider society, yet such racial inequalities exist as a backdrop to convivial life (Gilroy, 2004, p. xi). In many ways, this is what young Danish Muslims are demonstrating. They could live convivially in very diverse spaces, yet these spaces do not detract from the increasing ethnonationalism that has been on the rise in Danish society and has affected these youth's early childhood and youthhood.

---

2 Common housing in Denmark is not-for-profit rental flats, which make up around 20% of Denmark's housing stock.

82   *Muslim Pathways and Spatial Narratives*

Challenging Social Perception: Constructing an Affluent Self-Image

Khadija[3] was a 21-year-old woman and a first-year university student. She was one of the most internationally connected of my Danish interlocutors. As a child, she had attended international schools, and while she came to Denmark when she was only 2 years old, a few years later at 7 years old, her family moved to her parents' country of origin, where she lived for 8 years. Growing up, her father was a successful entrepreneur, and so, although they lived in a rental apartment in a working-class neighbourhood in Copenhagen, they had a comfortable lifestyle that enabled her parents to pay for her international schooling. Khadija's transnational life history meant that most of her friends had also attended international schools and as such came from affluent families.

Both in her city tour and our 3-hour-long interview, Khadija's self-representation was a contestation of the racialisation of the Muslim Other as socioeconomically and culturally inferior. Khadija perceived herself as the complete opposite to this image. In contrast, she hung out with an affluent crowd, went to trendy upscale cafes and restaurants, and would not spend much time in Nørrebro, which in her view—and in colloquial representation— characterised a social class different from hers. Nevertheless, we started our tour in *Kaffehuset* (the Coffee House) at the edge of the trendy part of Nørrebro. This area was previously a red segment on the map (Figure 4.1), but now increasingly green, signifying a change in socioeconomic and ethnic/racial demographics as young (white) professionals move to this part of town. The café was relatively new at the time. It had beautiful murals on one of the walls, antique quaint furniture, and attracted young people similar to Khadija: socially mobile, ethnically diverse, and who could afford the comforts of hanging out at coffee shops (Figure 4.3).

> We are on Nørrebrogade [no.] 25, which is 20 minutes away from my house on bike. I sometimes come here to meet my friends for coffee, because it's not far from my house. Either we study, I've come here a couple of times for work and meetings and stuff like that. It's chill and low-key. I bike here, I like biking around Copenhagen. It's fairly new, I think it's a group of guys who own it. [...]
>   *Is this area [Nørrebro] not Important to you?*
>   No, I don't relate too much to *Nørrebrogade*, I just come here because it's close. It's usually *Nyhavn* and *Kongens Nytorv*. There's a salad place I really like to eat at and then the *Kongelige Teater* and just walk around there. And then usually, I'm at friends' houses or at home.
>   (Khadija, Copenhagen)

---

3 Khadija's tour was conducted in English, so all quotes are *ad verbatim* transcripts.

Contesting Racialised Spaces in Copenhagen 83

Figure 4.3 Picture of the inside of *Kaffehuset*.

Our meeting point for Khadija's tour was outside *Kaffehuset*,[4] a coffee place on Nørrebro Street a short bike ride from her home. It is worth noting that on her route to this café she passed by several other coffee shops. She did not explain her choice in much detail, but it is noteworthy that three other participants took me to this same café. The café is located at the edge of Nørrebro, bordering the Queen Louise bridge that leads to downtown Copenhagen. This is the part of Nørrebro that has a trendy vibe, and as another interlocutor explained, the trendy vibe ends at "the yellow wall" (see Figure 4.2).

"The yellow wall" is a well-known landmark that borders a cemetery—*Assistentens Kirkegård*—where many of Denmark's cultural icons are buried. According to this young woman, anything north of 'the yellow wall' is less trendy and represents a more stereotypical version of working-class socially deprived Nørrebro. This section of Nørrebro is represented by the large red sections of the "socioeconomic" map (Figure 4.1) showing where racialised Others live—all of whom are categorised as "non-Westerners" in public imaginary, political discourse, and, more importantly, in policy documents pertaining to gentrification efforts in parts of the city. These policies—popularly known as the "ghetto laws" (Overgaard, 2020)—have sought to change the demographic make-up of

---

4 The location of *Kaffehuset* has since changed ownership and name.

84   *Muslim Pathways and Spatial Narratives*

Nørrebro (and other culturally diverse neighbourhoods) from over 50% "non-Western" working-class residents to white middle-class residents. In Denmark, politicians and policy administrators make little pretense of the racist intentions underlying their gentrification policies (Regeringen, 2018). The political discourses thus directly refer to "non-Westerners" in policy strategies aimed at changing the demographic (read: racial) make-up of certain urban neighbourhoods. Because of these policies, this area of Nørrebro has experienced rapid change with a greater influx of white middle-class professionals moving in, and thus does not have the same stigma it used to have.

Walking away from Nørrebro, Khadija took me to downtown Copenhagen, the next stop on her tour. The smaller streets in downtown Copenhagen are well known for their hip cafes and bars. The people on the streets looked young, affluent, and white Danish. Because of Khadija's international school background, she did not have many white Danish friends. Nevertheless, most of her friends were affluent, belonging to a different social position than what most of Nørrebro represented to Khadija. Understanding the hegemonic representation of Nørrebro as socioeconomically inferior, Khadija's hesitation to associate herself with Nørrebro makes sense. Nørrebro is anything but affluent; it is more closely linked with youth subcultural trends representing both leftist and minority cultural trends. As such, this district has historically attracted a bohemian artistic culture along with the working-class immigrant and marginalised citizens of Copenhagen. This is, however, slowly changing since 2018 as capital investment, gentrification efforts, and state regulation of common housing areas are pushing poor and racialised residents out of Nørrebro, replacing them with more socioeconomically secure (presumably white) residents.

Khadija's self-perception becomes more apparent as we walk towards *Nyhavn*, and she explains her love for high culture (Figure 4.4).

> The Royal Theatre had a summer show, I went to [it] and they showed the previews of the shows. So, I already know what shows I want to go see. I wish I could go more often, but it is so expensive and I'm a student. There was a stage and we were sitting on the grass. And, I like jazz and Frank Sinatra, so they have a show called "Fly Away" that I really wanted to go see, but it was too late. My high school friend [X], we decided to become each other's culture buddies, she also just finished her BA in social sciences. I'm in my first year.
>
> [We pass by a street musician playing "What a Wonderful World", and Khadija hums along] I like this atmosphere … It's sitting outside, it's chilling, it's nice.
>
> (Khadija, Copenhagen)

Figure 4.4 Advert from the Royal Theatre hanging on *Kongens Nytorv*.

As we walked, Khadija talked about her appreciation of musical expression, including ballet, opera, and jazz—all affluent art forms in Denmark.[5] Humming along to "What a Wonderful World," Khadija tactfully opposed the perception of inner-city Muslim youth as less exposed to (white) high culture. It is often assumed that youth who grow up in the working-class suburbs of Copenhagen in general are not exposed to high culture; Muslim and non-Muslim alike. Khadija chose to show me sites that represented a rebuttal of this often racialised stereotype, demonstrating instead her appreciation with a world very different from her working-class neighbourhood in the northwest of Copenhagen. The ballet ad-posters on *Kongens Nytorv* provided her a narrative opportunity to discretely position herself within an affluent social class. The only challenge was her lack of funds to afford this lifestyle. Pointing out her friend's house in the middle of *Nyhavn*, one of the most exclusive addresses in Copenhagen, highlighted Khadija's positioning even further. The next few stops on her tour further established her affluent self-image (Figure 4.5).

---

5 While jazz originated as part of Black musical culture in the US rooted in experiences of racist socioeconomic marginalisation, this history has not been translated into the Danish jazz scene. Danish jazz often attracts a white middle-aged and middle-class audience. This is contrary to more contemporary forms of US Black hip-hop, rap and R&B music that is more widely consumed among racialised youth in Denmark.

86 *Muslim Pathways and Spatial Narratives*

Figure 4.5 Hotel D'Angleterre, Copenhagen.

> This is D'Angleterre. It's a really fancy hotel. I've never been, but me and my friend have a deal; if I'm 25 and I'm not married, we'll have a dinner there. Here or *Den Sorte Diamant* [The Black Diamond, the Royal Library], there's a really nice restaurant there.
>
> (Khadija, Copenhagen)

Khadija showed me three sites she identified with her "imagined" self: the Royal Theatre, the Opera House, and Hotel D'Angleterre. Khadija was not intimately familiar with any of these sites. In fact, she had never been inside any of them. Yet, they demonstrated a lifestyle Khadija aspired to. She wished she had the financial capacity to make these sites a part of her life—to live a life of middle-class comfort. This was not a farfetched dream for Khadija; she was a first-year university student with good employment prospects when she graduated. Thus, planning a birthday dinner at D'Angleterre when she turned 25 was not unrealistic. This would be a time in her life when she had graduated university, was working fulltime, and had a decent income and no dependants.

Her appreciation of ballet and opera, and her love for exclusive cafes and restaurants, all created a narrative of affluence. It became an implicit contestation of the racialised (female) Muslim Other. During her interview, Khadija was in fact very explicit about how she struggled to identify with the existing racialisation of the hijab-wearing woman from Nørrebro. Her hijab

Contesting Racialised Spaces in Copenhagen   87

emphasised her Muslimness; however, so although not made explicit during our walk, her spatial narrative presented a way of challenging this image of inferiority.

Khadija's spatial narrative addresses an omnipresent white Danish gaze, which is always looking at her and evaluating her (Khawaja, 2011). Throughout her tour, it was difficult to escape this racialising gaze. Perhaps it did not help that we were walking in a White space—to use Elijah Anderson's concept (2022)—with very few racialised Others. Khadija was not just taking *me* around her Copenhagen. She was constructing a counter-narrative against the racialisation of Muslims imagined by a hegemonic white gaze. Khadija constructed an *imagined* self through these spaces that conveniently rooted her within spaces perceived as predominately white. Whether conscious or not, there was a tactic to Khadija's spatial narrative; a capacity to navigate the urban terrain to write an alternative story to the otherisation of the Muslim Other. She did this by rooting herself within spaces that rejected her belonging. The reality was that Khadija was not far from living the comfortable lifestyle that she could not currently afford. Being part of the small elite of young Muslims in Copenhagen enrolled in higher education, Khadija could easily make a comfortable middle-class wage in a few years and would belong to a higher social position of Muslims. This affluent association was not unique to Khadija but represented most of my Danish interlocutors' tours to different degrees.

Creating a Copenhagener Self-Image through City Spaces

Dania was a 22-year-old young woman, born and raised in a rural town on Funen island (*Fyn*). She moved to Copenhagen when she started university and had since adopted the city as her home. She did not see herself ever moving back to her rural childhood town. In this regard, Dania followed the typical stream of rural-urban migrants who are moving from rural areas in Jutland and Funen to the capital for higher education and professional opportunities (Sørensen, 2015). Dania's appreciation for Copenhagen's cultural diversity and the lifestyle it allowed her became clear in her tour as she took me to her favourite shops and streets in Nørrebro. While Khadija's tour aimed at constructing an affluent self-image through city spaces, Dania took me on a tour to depict an *urban* self-image, as opposed to her rural background.

We met near Blågårdsplads, a side street to Nørrebrogade. This street had been a hub for criminal activity just a few years prior . However, Blågårdsplads has gone through massive gentrification with trendy restaurants, cafés, and vintage clothing stores opening, attracting young Danes seeking a more "authentic urban" experience. The charm of Blågårdsplads lies in its cultural diversity and its urban history. It gives the street character, attracting people seeking an escape from the commercialism that dominates the high streets of Copenhagen. Dania belonged to this segment; as a young university student

88 Muslim Pathways and Spatial Narratives

from Funen, she sought out the excitement and diversity of Nørrebro. She had turned Nørrebro and Blågårdsplads into her home turf rather than her more affluent Frederiksberg address (the unmarked circle on the map, see Figure 4.1). The borough of Frederiksberg neighbours Nørrebro, but it is socially better off. It is a rich borough with a less multicultural vibe yet still young and trendy. Dania explained that she did not really feel connected to Frederiksberg in the same way she did with Nørrebro. Nørrebro had become the hub of her social and volunteer life. The first stop on her tour was at the humanitarian NGO, where she volunteered (Figure 4.6).

> [We enter the NGO's office, and Dania introduces me to the volunteers] It's a cozy workplace. I volunteer here. This is the main office where we have our volunteer meetings. I've organized volunteer events, I've helped a lot with humanitarian [dinner events], where we get dinner sponsored and collect donations.
>
> Many of us come here, not because we are eager to do Islamic [volunteer] work. I think I'm very passionate about humanitarianism and helping others, and that's my entire [social] network. Because it is my closest friends who work here. So, you meet up and hang out and work together rather than meeting as a bunch of different people who don't know each other. When you know each other so well, it feels like a small community.
>
> (Dania, Copenhagen)

Figure 4.6 Inside the NGO office where Dania volunteers.

Dania took me inside the offices of the NGO, showed me around, and introduced me to the volunteers and the general secretary, who were working in the office. The NGO had a bookshop selling Islamic books, toys, and prayer mats, and a second-hand clothing store across the street. Dania first started volunteering in the second-hand store every Saturday and later continued to volunteer at the main office. The NGO was a small-scale organisation where everyone knew each other intimately, contrary to other mainstream NGOs in the area.

Similar to Khadija, Dania did not feel a need to emphasise her Muslimness to me; her hijab was a clear enough symbol of that. What mattered to Dania was to demonstrate what was important to her: volunteering, ethnically diverse grocery stores, and urban life. Nørrebro represented this to her (Figure 4.7).

The next stop on her tour was a stroll through *Blågårdsplads* [Blågårds Square]:

> This is Blågård Square. I spend most of my time on this street, this walk we're going on now. I shop a lot, but I don't think it's relevant for your project to take you shopping, because that is not where I unfold my Muslim identity. [I do that] more in this context. [It's not] just my Muslim, but also my other ethnic background [*anden etnisk baggrund*] that is more expressed here than it is where I live in Frederiksberg. I don't spend any time there [in Frederiksberg]. I have a nice park right

Figure 4.7 Blågård Square (*Blågårdsplads*), Nørrebro.

90 *Muslim Pathways and Spatial Narratives*

next to me, I've been there twice. It's just not a place [for me]. This [Nørrebro] is where I go with my friends. We'll go by a cafe, where I'm taking you to now, walk over to the NGO, greet people, sit and grab a coffee with [the general secretary], chat a bit, go to the Danish Islamic Centre [mosque]. So, this walk, I come here once or twice a week, do grocery shopping, Arabic vegetables. I bike through here. Halal meat, I buy here perhaps once a month. [I] buy vegetables, squash, if I want a good *sameh* [Palestinian dish], which is stuffed squash with meat and rice. I can't get that at *Fakta* [Danish discount grocery store]. *Lubia* [wide green beens], *bamiya* [okra], lentils. So, it's also here food-wise that I get to express myself. Food, like *Ahaaa* [Middle Eastern restaurant], that's popular Palestinian food, it's one of the most student friendly places. They have it here [on Blågård Street] and on Nørrebro Street, I mostly come here because it's more local, where the other [Ahaaa] is fancier.

(Dania, Copenhagen)

While we were walking through Blågårdsplads, Dania explained how this street was not just a representation of her Muslim identity but a place where she could express her "other ethnic background." "Other ethnic background" is a political categorisation of non-white Danes, which precluded the label "non-Westerners." These labels, including "second-generation immigrants," "new Danes," and the increasingly more popular distinction of "Muslims," are all part of a racialising hegemonic discourse that differentiates between white Danes and Danes of colour. What Dania presents in this extract is how internalised this categorisation has become, not necessarily in negative terms, but here Dania identifies herself not only with her particular ethnicity (although this was also important to her) but in fact sees herself and her cultural expressions as part of this whole group of racialised Others (across ethnic and cultural diversities).

Dania took me to one of her favourite Middle Eastern grocery stores located at the end of Blågårdsplads (Figure 4.8).

I want to show you the grocery store here, because I come here often or the one down at Nørrebro station. There's also a grocery store there that has a wider selection and cheaper prices. I want to say that this [Blågård Street] is a very hip place for non-Muslim Danes. The good thing about a place like this are these types of vegetables that I use: *mujadara* and *couscous* and *knafa* [different Middle Eastern dishes]. It's funny, this smells like home [the smell of spices coming from the grocery store] but this [points at the flowers and cafes across the street] also smells like home.

(Dania, Copenhagen)

Figure 4.8 Grocery store in Blågårds Square, Nørrebro.

It seemed random as we looked through the crammed aisles of dried legumes and assortments of rice and other imported goods. However, every now and then, Dania would draw my attention to a particular item, demonstrating her own fascination with finding these items so close to home, yet so far away from their origin.

In many ways, Dania's city did not represent her history of growing up in rural Denmark. It was not an autobiographical journey through the streets she had made her own either. Her tour was a construction of a certain version of herself. Besides being Muslim, Palestinian, and from rural Funen, Dania was also a Copenhagener living in Frederiksberg and biking her way through the urban streets of Nørrebro—or rather, the charming side of Nørrebro that had just the right balance of urban living, trendy cafes, and Middle Eastern stores.

Dania took me to Elmegade, a side street to Nørrebro, almost opposite to Blågårdsplads. Several other participants also took me to Elmegade; this is a small street full of independent Danish fashion designers and unique stores and cafes. To me, it represented the bohemian-turned-hipster version of Nørrebro that attracts young leftist (white) Danish professionals and a wish to escape the fast fashion franchises of the Copenhagen high street. The clothes on display on this street still followed the Danish fashion convention of a monochrome colour palette and simple design. As we passed by one of these clothing displays, Dania commented on her own style of dress (Figure 4.9).

92 *Muslim Pathways and Spatial Narratives*

Figure 4.9 Store window on Elmegade, Nørrebro.

I wear Western clothes a lot because I think clothes really symbolise who you are. I've chosen not to wear *abaya* (Middle Eastern-style long dress) consciously, and that's because it just doesn't fit with the sort of person I am. So, I also shop in Scandinavian shops. I find it's really important that there's a balance. The reason I've come to this street [Elmegade], is because there's a lot of local designers, so the clothes you buy here, some of it is hand sewn and there's only [the items] that are in the shop. Something like that [the dress in the middle on the picture] with a pair of black jeans and sandals. That's what I like about this street – it's small-scale entrepreneurs that have opened their own [store].

(Dania, Copenhagen)

Dania explained a conscious effort to represent herself through her clothing choices. She chose not to wear an *abaya* and preferred instead to buy clothes in Scandinavian stores. Even when it came to her choice of hijab-style, she would only choose to wear certain colours and simple designs. She took me to one of her favourite hijab shops, where she explained how she would choose earth-coloured and simple-toned shawls, staying true to the Scandinavian aesthetic palette of simplicity and inconspicuous colours.

Figure 4.10 Large mural in *Kaffehuset*, Nørrebro.

There is an important point in Dania's emphasis on what sort of clothes she chooses to wear; a point shared by other Muslim women when talking about their styles of clothes. The hypervisibility of being a Muslim woman wearing a hijab has meant that Dania puts a lot of thought into the type of clothes and colours she wears and how well it blends into the streets of Copenhagen. While an *abaya* did not represent who she was, a handsewn, locally sourced dress from a store on Elmegade localises and roots Dania within her urban context. In other words, Dania implicitly challenges the perceived foreignness of her Muslimness by localising its style within a Scandinavian aesthetic. There is an important tactical element in these seemingly superficial choices that challenges the unescapable label of "foreignness" by localising it within the urbanscape, making it less conspicuous.

For the next stop on her tour, Dania took me to *Kaffehuset* that is located on Nørrebrogade, almost between Elmegade and Blågårdsgade. It is the same café in which I met Khadija, and which several other participants took me to as well (Figures 4.10 and 4.11).

> This is *Kaffehuset*. It was actually a *Baresso* [a Danish franchise coffee place similar to Starbucks] before they sold it. So, it's the same type of interior design. I think that mural is so beautiful. We usually sit here on this, we call it the grandmother-couch, it's like a little

Figure 4.11 Quant antique furniture in *Kaffehuset*, Nørrebro.

grandmother-living room. This is where we usually sit when we have meetings with the [NGO second-hand store], and then we're all just gathered around this little table.

(Dania, Copenhagen)

With its welcoming atmosphere, it was easy to imagine how the café attracted the young people I met for work, study, and socialising. When visiting this popular café, several youth would mention the owners. Dania explained that the owners were a group of friends who were happy to sponsor the NGO's meetings, and another participant mentioned that they were Muslim. In either case, the owners seemed to represent something more than just café owners. They were local Muslim Copenhageners, whose café represented something that my interlocutors identified with; it was trendy, upscale, and halal. Although my interlocutors, Dania included, did not exclusively go to Muslim-owned restaurants and cafes, the fact that *Kaffehusets* owners' religious background kept becoming part of the narrative is noteworthy. *Kaffehuset* did not look "multicultural". In fact, it looked like any other non-franchise coffee shop in Copenhagen. It is perhaps this inconspicuousness that appealed to my Danish participants. *Kaffehuset* was a representation of what it meant to be a young, successful Muslim Copenhagener.

Contesting Racialised Spaces in Copenhagen 95

Figure 4.12 Inside *Assistentens* Cemetery, Nørrebro.

Dania's last stop on her tour was *Assistentens Kirkegård* [The Assistant's Cemetery], behind "the yellow wall". We walked into the cemetery and Dania took me on a picturesque walk through the garden (Figure 4.12).

> This is behind the yellow wall – *Assistentens Kirkegård*. People use it as a park. It may be that there are dead people lying around everywhere, but people use it as a park. It's very normal culture here in Nørrebro. I would buy an ice cream and walk through the cemetery. It's a long path and then there's trees all the way and you don't see the tombs.
>
> (Dania, Copenhagen)

The walk through the cemetery was serene and calm, sheltered from the busy high street of Nørrebro. As we walked, Dania commented on how people— herself included—used the cemetery as a park that offered an escape from the stress of urban life. We sat down on a bench near Natasha Saad's (reggae musician) and Dan Turell's (fiction author/poet) graves. Despite her mother's shock over her taking casual strolls through a cemetery, Dania explained that "it's not like you think about the fact that it's a *cemetery*." The grave plots seemed to be mere accessories to a beautiful oasis of large trees and calmness in the city centre. As we sat there in the afternoon summer sun, Dania ended her city tour, stopping behind the yellow wall; not venturing beyond this point to the other side of Nørrebro.

96   *Muslim Pathways and Spatial Narratives*

Dania was born and raised in rural Denmark. She is one of many Danish youth escaping rural life for city centres such as Copenhagen and Aarhus for higher education and work opportunities. Dania's tour did not focus on how Copenhagen had become her home through the years, but rather how the sites were ways in which she wanted to represent herself. The tour was about constructing a spatial representation of self— and in Dania's case, this meant including sites that demonstrated everything that defined her as Muslim, Danish, Palestinian, and "ethnic Other." It was more than that, however; her tour was about how she saw herself as a young university student who had developed through the years from being a young rural girl in a big city to becoming an urbanite with social and cultural capital allowing her to seamlessly become part of the trendy parts of Nørrebro's urbanscape.

Growing Up on the Other Side of the Yellow Wall

Khalid, whom I introduced in chapter 2, grew up on the wrong side of the yellow wall. The side my other participants did not want to include in their tours. The side of the city painted in red in Figure 4.1. In recent years, this area has become an important part of the government's 2018 housing policies introduced in this policy report *Ét Danmark uden parallelsamfund— Ingen ghettoer i 2030* [One Denmark without parallel societies—No ghettos in 2030] (Regeringen, 2018). The policies aim to rapidly change the racial make-up of residents and introduce various gentrifying efforts that target and potentially displace racialised and poor residents.

In his wide-ranging tour, Khalid put his life and current social mobility in an autobiographical context, complexifying the image of the "wrong" side of Nørrebro and challenging its hegemonic representation in popular imaginary as divorced from wider Danish society, socioeconomically marginalised, and quintessentially Other. For Khalid, life on this side of Nørrebro had a personal significance to his current life and success. This part of Nørrebro was an important place in his spatial narrative, but before going there, we had to take a detour to his university, workplace, and mosque—setting the tone of the narrative to emphasise social position and mobility. In fact, Khalid's spatial narrative stressed how it was the local opportunities of his neighbourhood as well as his childhood friends that helped motivate him to recognise his own potential. With these sites, he was constructing a version of himself that challenged the racialised representation of young Muslim men living in inner-Nørrebro as prone to delinquency.

Our meeting place for Khalid's tour was the new central mosque in Copenhagen. We met right after Friday prayer outside the mosque; this was the first site on his tour. Khalid walked me through the new mosque, showing off its beautiful features and facilities (Figure 4.13).

This place [the mosque] recently opened, two months ago, just before Ramadan, and I've used it every day, for some of the prayers at least.

Contesting Racialised Spaces in Copenhagen 97

Figure 4.13 Inside Hamad Bin Khalifa Mosque, Nørrebro.

So, it's been and is a part of my daily life, especially because I go to school close by and I live not far from here. It's all close by.

(Khalid, Copenhagen)

Khalid seemed proud to show off the mosque. From the *wudu* (ablution) area to the conference rooms and library, he noted what a rare sight it was to see in a Danish mosque. Other participants also commented on the importance of this new and modern mosque. It seemed to be a long-awaited landmark of their belonging to Copenhagen and, by extension Denmark. Other Muslim youth may not have used this grand mosque as much as Khalid; however, it was a stamp of their presence in the city's landscape.

Next stop on Khalid's tour was his part-time position as a consultant at a prestigious company just a 10-minute drive away. The company was located in one of the most exclusive addresses by the Copenhagen harbour in Hellerup (Figure 4.14).

It's a very classy area. It's not at all what I'm used to in Nørrebro, I can assure you that. Sometimes you get some weird looks. People thought I was out-of-place. I've gotten looks from people who thought, what is this guy doing here. But most people have been nice about it. I think I'm the youngest person working here as well. It's funny, there's two immigrants or Muslims who work here, there's me and then someone from

98 *Muslim Pathways and Spatial Narratives*

Figure 4.14 Inside the office building where Khalid works in Hellerup, Copenhagen.

[the mosque]. I've had lunch with him a few times. But there aren't a lot of Muslims here. It's been a bit easier to be one of the few Muslims here, because people usually draw on their personal experiences with Muslims. Like, here in the beginning of Ramadan, one of them said to me: "Well Khalid, are you going to fast? I knew someone, he had to get drunk before fasting in Ramadan." You have to think about it, of course there's 2 billion Muslims and we're not all the same. [By being one of the few Muslims,] I don't have to be considerate about what they think about other Muslims doing this or that. It's my daily life, if they don't like me praying there, they can look out the window [laughs]. I do my job and that's what I'm hired to do.

(Khalid, Copenhagen)

Khalid made a point to emphasise how his workplace differed from his life in Nørrebro. His workplace was much more upscale. He described getting looks from people who probably thought he looked out-of-place because of his ethnicity, although they were polite about it. Being one of the youngest employees simply added to his colleagues' curiosity. Khalid's description of being out-of-place says more about his *feeling* out-of-place than the actual reactions he received from colleagues. He was young and one of only two Muslims in the whole multi-company building. There is something significant in his self-description as "immigrants or Muslims" that directs our

Contesting Racialised Spaces in Copenhagen   99

attention to an external gaze (Khawaja, 2011). Khalid would describe himself as Muslim in other contexts too, but within this framing it was not the self-identification that mattered but rather the feeling of otherisation within a White space that he was alluding to (Anderson, 2022).

As we walked around his workplace neighbourhood, Khalid pointed out the expensive apartments and the view of the Øresund Bridge connecting Denmark and Sweden. He continued to explain his discomfort with social mobility. It was not an easy process and required him to step out of his Nørrebro comfort zone:

> I feel comfortable in this area [of my workplace] when I'm at work. [I'm] also dressed in professional clothes, but it's not really me. You feel most at home where you've lived your whole life and where you grew up. But you have to leave your comfort zone to gain success in life. In a way it's been difficult, because you've experienced barriers, but it wasn't difficult to get [a job] out here. I got the job when I was doing an internship at [X] right next to where I live. The new [manager there] still had a lot of connections in the industry, so I spoke with her about doing an internship in the industry. I told her: "Please help me get the right connections, because you know I don't have those connections. A lot of people have families who work in companies etc., I just don't have that. And you know I have the potential to do a good job, so help me out." So she called someone who works up there [at the consultancy agency], one of the most leading in the field, who was her friend. Then they called me and invited me for an interview, and I went on vacation and started working there right after.
>
> (Khalid, Copenhagen)

Accompanying Khalid, as he walked me through the large open reception area of the building, I immediately empathised with his experience as I embodied my own experience of feeling out-of-place in the space. As we were standing in the large reception hall, Khalid took the opportunity to compare his workplace with his inner-city neighbourhood. It is in this comparison that Khalid displayed his own awkwardness with his change of social position; he was no longer an inner-city brown kid fighting against common stereotypes of Muslim young men. Instead, he was an accepted part of a professional work environment where he was a qualified employee. And yet, he still felt he was invading a space to which he was not entitled, he needed to dress the part and live up to the performance of an "acceptable professional." The idea of Khalid "invading" an affluent professional space draws on the work of Nirmal Puwar and her conceptualisation of woman and racialised others as *space invaders*. This concept emphasises how racialised others disrupt white spaces when they attempt to become socially, professionally, or politically part of these spaces and thus have to find ways of managing their otherness

100 *Muslim Pathways and Spatial Narratives*

within these spaces (Puwar, 2004). In Khalid's case, he had to dress and perform the part.

Khalid got his current position through his social capital. Being able to network with his internship supervisor, he was conscious of his need to be proactive in promoting his competencies. He played on the stereotype that Nørrebro kids like him, from disadvantaged neighbourhoods, did not have a professional network in the same way middle-class white Danes may have. The fact of the matter was, however, Khalid's social network was predominantly comprised of young professionals who also grew up in inner-Nørrebro. He and his network of friends were well-equipped to achieve social mobility contrary to the stereotypical image of a racialised Muslim man from disadvantaged neighbourhoods. Nevertheless, Khalid was conscious of this stereotype. While he did not internalise this perception, he did tactically employ it to benefit from his supervisor's gatekeeping. It was because of his social navigation skills that Khalid knew how to approach her, highlighting his competencies and professional ambitions. This seemed to be a recurring theme among my Danish interlocutors. They saw their own potential to achieve a higher level of social mobility in comparison to their working-class neighbourhoods, and they were not hesitant to display this self-image to me.

As we started to leave his workplace, Khalid explained his perspective on success and the importance of creating a good professional impression:

> There's a good story about *Sayedna* Yusuf [Prophet Josef], when he was asked by the king if he could come interpret the dream, he said yes, he didn't hesitate. You must step up when you need to. You also must make an effort. You must build relationships, and that's what I did with my [supervisor]. Initially, she didn't like me and didn't want to hire me [after my internship]. But I made a good impression and was open with her, when we spoke about our private life, so they also know that you're a person. The [supervisor] definitely had her prejudice that had to be taken down slowly.
>
> (Khalid, Copenhagen)

In this description, Khalid highlights the difficulties that exist when having to deal with the racialisation of Muslim men in the workplace. As a Muslim male, Khalid had to respond to his supervisor's prejudices against him to develop a better rapport with her. This meant that he had to be sensitive and take the time to answer her questions about his personal and religious life. He explained how disproving people's preconceived notions about him was a matter of fact. Khalid had been sensible and strategic in developing good professional relationships, yet he could not escape the omnipresent white gaze that both Khadija and Dina spoke of as well. All their spatial narratives were constructed through racialised spaces in which they could not escape their visibility as Muslim Others.

Contesting Racialised Spaces in Copenhagen 101

Khalid's spatial narrative had largely bypassed the social issues usually attributed to this section of Nørrebro, i.e. "beyond the yellow wall." Showing me his version of inner-Nørrebro highlighted the discrepancy between his social position and the stereotype that was usually attributed to young men resembling him in this area. This side of Nørrebro was an area several interlocutors did not want to identify with because of the social stigma connected to it. However, Khalid wanted to display what this side of Nørrebro meant to him and how it was an essential part of how he had come to see himself. Nørrebro—north of the yellow wall—may represent problematic social issues in political and media representation and thus excuse heightened surveillance by public institutions. Nevertheless, to Khalid and his neighbourhood friends, this neighbourhood was a catalyst for realising the potential they had discovered at their local sports club. Khalid's self-image was constructed on this basis—he was never a troubled youth needing to be supported by inner-city initiatives and role models. Rather, he had been surrounded by people cheering for him since his early childhood, distinguishing himself from the dominant racialised perception of Muslim inferiority. His city tour was a representation of the actualisation of this potential into social mobility; starting with where he was in his life now, working at a prestigious company while finishing his postgraduate degree, and ending his tour with where it all began in his childhood neighbourhood in inner-Nørrebro.

Spatial Narratives as Creative Navigation

The Copenhagen municipality map (Figure 4.1) represents the city in relation to the socioeconomic division of space and how this division is understood in racialised terms. My interlocutors did not need to see this map to perceive what this division of space meant in social terms. In this regard, it is useful to think of Henri Lefebvre's (2014) conceptualisation of the various processes through which social space is produced, perceived, and represented. The spatial narratives presented in this chapter demonstrate how these processes of spatialisation allow opportunities but also limitations for racialised Others to navigate and contest their otherisation in spatial terms. It is in the Copenhagen map that the racialisation of "non-Westerners" as socioeconomically inferior is quite literally written into space and reproduced in public consciousness. Understanding these racialised representations, the young Muslims I met knew how to tactically navigate through the city spaces, challenging the perceptions of Muslim belonging and rooting themselves within spaces perceived as hegemonically white spaces.

In chapter 2, I highlighted how Danish Muslims experienced and reacted to political and media discourses on ethnic and religious minorities and how these discourses affected everyday interactions. It is important to understand Danish Muslims' experiences of racialisation processes that have become increasingly popular in Danish political discourses. However, there are other ways of understanding processes of racialisation that go beyond the focus of

102 *Muslim Pathways and Spatial Narratives*

the political structures and instead look at social actors' agency to contest representations of inferiority. Shifting the analytical gaze to young Muslims' spatial agency emphasises how they tactically utilise spaces to create an alternative narrative of the Danish Muslim as highly achieving, successful urban dwellers rooted in the city's spaces. These tactics can be understood as a contestation of the hegemonic narrative about Muslim citizens, which, as we see with the map in the chapter's introduction, is translated into spatial terms and dominates the colloquial understanding of the (racialised) class divisions of city spaces.

The different spaces in Copenhagen that my interlocutors took me to represent the hierarchical differentiation they attributed to the city. Some places were deemed fashionable, trendy, and "authentically urban," while others had a lingering connotation of social deprivation. These spatial representations are what Lefebvre refers to in his theorisation of the production of social space. These young Muslims attributed particular social meaning to the spaces around them. They thus made distinct choices in their city tours. It is through these movements that they creatively manipulated the hidden potentials within societal structures to claim a pathway towards self-expression and social mobility. In other words, the creativity presented in their movements and narratives through the city was neither entirely random nor completely preconceived. Rather, these navigational tactics are an expression of creative improvisation. According to John Liep, cultural creativity can be understood as the production of "something new through the recombination and transformation of existing cultural practices or forms" (Liep, 2001, p. 2). In the context of the spatial narratives presented in this chapter, the question revolves around how and why young Danish Muslims chose certain city spaces rather than others to represent themselves. Ingold and Hallam argue improvisation is creativity through process; in other words, "the objective is thus to look at the movements that create creativity" in improvisation (Hallam & Ingold, 2021, pp. 2–3). The concept of improvisation thus focuses on how my participants negotiate the social connotations of particular spaces vis-à-vis their own social position.

Amit and Knowles (2017) further developed the theorisation of improvisation in relation to mobility by suggesting using the concept of tacking to connect the concepts of navigation and improvisation with different processes of mobility. Re-conceptualising the nautical term of tacking, Amit and Knowles highlight how the concept focuses on "a process of ongoing adjustment" (2017, p. 3). The ability to change course and adjust to circumstances requires knowledge, experience, and improvisation (ibid.). In the context of Copenhagen, young Danish Muslims' deep knowledge of the different districts, their life experiences in these areas, and the social connotations they knew these areas represented enabled them to effortlessly navigate these spaces to improvise a narrative they wanted to represent. A narrative that emphasised their social mobility, their resources, and their embeddedness in the city. Amit and Knowles argue that "[n]avigation shapes the character of space and how we might think about it, through the movements and objects of routes: what passes through a street, a neighbourhood, a city, co-constitutes it" (2017, p. 11). My Danish participants thus transformed the Copenhagen landscape through their navigations. In turn, through their movements, they enabled Copenhagen to strategically formulate its urban identity as a culturally diverse global city.

Walking with my interlocutors and emphasising the social significance they attribute to particular spaces reveal how spatial narratives can become important avenues for understanding the interplay between social actors and structures. The ways in which these youth improvised their movements and narratives demonstrate how improvisation is both retrospective and prospective (Amit & Knowles, 2017, p. 6). Their ability to improvise and construct a spatial representation of self required a social knowledge of the city spaces that predated their tour. Their choices of movements were not unreflective but rather demonstrated a deep social knowledge and experience with the city. It is important to distinguish between the tours these youth took me on and how they inhabit the city. In other words, their tours were not necessarily an image of their everyday movements. Rather, they projected an image of these young adults' social mobility and position vis-à-vis the racialised representation of Muslims that prevailed in Danish political and media discourses. At the same time, their tours also depicted an image of Copenhagen as a diverse city that embraced the cultural differences that my interlocutors represented.

Conclusion

The socioeconomic map I introduced in the beginning of this chapter seemed to be a dominant (political) perception of how "non-Westerners" (who are racialised as Muslims in political and popular imaginary in Denmark) are equated with "signs of socioeconomic marginalisation" alongside other markers such as unemployment and income levels. These racial and class markers permeate the urban spaces and become an omnipresent spatial framework my interlocutors navigated through as they created spatial narratives. Thus, their spatial narratives cannot be disconnected from political and social processes of racialisation. It is this which makes processes of racialisation and spatialisation interconnected.

This became apparent as my interlocutors always seemed to be walking and talking against something—a grand narrative that painted them in a picture they were eager to correct. There was a lingering omnipresence of white hegemony that seemed to judge them as we walked through Copenhagen's streets. It seemed they felt an urge to address this judgement and speak against it, although not calling it out for its racism. This is not to say that they did not have any agency in the narratives they constructed. Yet, agency in this regard, as mentioned in the Introduction, should be understood as a *capacity for action* within the limitations of a racialised social system. There

104 *Muslim Pathways and Spatial Narratives*

was a conscious tactic in taking me to some areas and avoiding others. The space became the text through which these young Muslims could emphasise their social position as "respectable *Danish* Muslims" rather than "inferior Muslim *Others.*" These young Danish Muslims thereby represented their Muslimness as a rooted part of Copenhagen's cultural diversity rather than a quintessential symbol of otherness.

5 Spatial Biographies and Rootedness in Montreal

This chapter focuses on Montreal Muslims' city walks, interrogating how processes of settlement and rootedness can be expressed through personal life histories as these intersect with particular city spaces. I focus on how my Montreal participants weave a spatial life narrative through the spaces they showed me. In the process, the spaces become autobiographical, enriched by nostalgic meaning, and highlighting important life moments. The chapter will explore concepts of rootedness as processual and dynamic, demonstrating how young Muslims are embedded into their urban spaces, and thus contribute to the spatialisation of the city by their presence and use of the city. Through their city walks, these youth wrote themselves into the history of their city. In doing so, they ingrained themselves within the city and inadvertently refuted the Quebec-nationalist rhetoric of the "Muslim Other."

The cases presented in the following depict spatial narratives that challenge the assumption of a "Muslim" monolith. By walking with young Muslims through their city spaces, I shifted my gaze from categorical and racialised signifiers (Muslim/immigrant/youth) to unique life narratives of settlement and rootedness in a city. Highlighting the particularities of my interlocutors' experiences, identifications, and outlooks, demonstrates the value of moving past *a priori* categorical determinations to investigate easily overlooked aspects of young Muslims' experiences when the focus is solely on processes of racialisation.

The young people I met in Montreal never spent much time or effort trying to convince me that they belonged in their city, province, or nation. They were already well-rooted in their city spaces, and they continued to develop these roots as their localities changed with economic and social restructuring. What happens when we stop assuming that young Muslims, whether migrant or not, are foreign to the societies they live in? What happens when we treat it as unexceptional that they live and relate locally—regardless of differences of dress, religious devotion, or summers spent in their parents' countries of origin? My Montreal participants all had different spaces they felt connected to through past experiences and memories. They took me on tours of *their* version of the city. Whether they had lived there for a few years or had been born and raised in the city, they all had a spatial narrative.

DOI: 10.4324/9781003294696-8

106   *Muslim Pathways and Spatial Narratives*

This chapter thus focuses on how my Montreal interlocutors rooted themselves in their locality through space, time, and memories. These memories connected them to the history of a certain place. They knew if a building had been renovated or if a street had been transformed, and they related it to their own memories of the sites. This chapter does not only demonstrate the rootedness of these young Montreal Muslims. It also highlights the more general temporal dimensions of city spaces and how they connect to personal biographies. Many of these youth were spatially mobile; they came from immigrant backgrounds, and their spatial connection to Montreal was coloured by their family's settlement. Nevertheless, there were some who were themselves migrants to the city, some international migrants but others rural–urban migrants, such as Amy, who had moved to Montreal from a small town in Ontario. The young Muslims' movements and different spatial biographies depict how diverse, nuanced, and distinguished their individual urban experiences are. They have different migration histories as well as socioeconomic circumstances, and their connections with different parts of Montreal are unique to their personal experiences. I explore how these youth weave a spatial life narrative through the spaces they showed me. In the process, the spaces become autobiographical, enriched by nostalgic meaning, and highlighting important life moments.

Navigating Urban Spaces and Constructing Spatial Biographies

In many ways, the unique migration histories of my participants only allow a limited understanding of their lives and connections to Montreal. Placing their experiences within migration literature that focuses on the processes of movement as larger journeys only provides a limited understanding of their lives in the city (Amit & Olwig, 2011). The more contemporary focus on mobility and its connection to smaller journeys as well as continuous journeys highlights the more nuanced experiences of many of the young Montrealers I met. The importance of locality and neighbourhood was ever-present in my fieldwork in Montreal. These youth only tangentially referred to their (or their family's) migration experiences in their spatial accounts. What mattered was the relationships with their city spaces and the pathways they had themselves constructed through these spaces.

In his classical essay on spatial and urban culture, Georg Simmel emphasises "the significance that the spatial conditions of a sociation possesses sociologically for other determinants and developments" (1997, p. 138). In this text, Simmel focuses on defining the different uses of space. It is only from understanding the use of space, he argues, that we come to understand what society may comprise of. An important point Simmel makes about space and distance is an emphasis on the psychological aspects of these concepts, thus arguing that it is not a physical proximity that binds people together, but rather the inhabitants of the spaces who attach social meaning to space. Simmel thus gives us a deeper theoretical basis for understanding the

Spatial Biographies and Rootedness in Montreal 107

relationship between physical and social space. The spatial accounts I present in this chapter demonstrate the social meaning my interlocutors attribute to their localities, whether through their life histories or social and emotional connections to particular spaces. Their journeys through their city are temporal connections. In other words, my interlocutors' spatial narratives connect time and space. These narratives demonstrate the meaning attributed to physical space through different times in their lives. The meaning the young Muslims narrated was constructed based on what they wanted to emphasise. For instance, they may have underplayed their parents' financial struggles and the challenges of settling in a new country, and instead emphasised the social life they enjoyed growing up in an inner-city neighbourhood.

The young adults that I present in this chapter all felt a strong connection to particular areas of Montreal and its suburbs. Nevertheless, their personal histories of migration and settlement in the city as well as their socioeconomic circumstances were very different. They had different starting points and possibilities of both spatial and social mobility in their cities. In many ways, these young people's spatial narratives force us to recognise the particularities in their experiences. This only became possible once I moved away from a categorical emphasis on their Muslim identification and the racialisation they experienced because of it. Moving away from this emphasis meant that I could explore their different experiences, identifications, prospects, and outlooks that they each had developed through their engagement with particular districts of Montreal. Rather than undermining their experiences of racialisation in both political discourse and everyday microaggressions, these young Muslims' spatial narratives became inadvertently convincing contestations of their Otherisation.

The process of settling in a new city and the social networks one develops in a city through the use of spaces are unique. It is through the unique spatial narratives that the cases in this chapter reveal the complexities of my interlocutors' individual experiences, attachments, and engagements with their city. As Caroline Knowles argues, "[people's] lives and subjectivities are about where they go and why, how they go, and who they encounter on the way" (2010, p. 376). Knowles further develops the connection between subjectivity and spatial biography in a article with Vered Amit. Here, they argue that spatial biography, i.e. narrating life stories through spaces, makes space "legible in its distinctiveness and through the navigational practices involved in negotiating it" (Amit & Knowles, 2017, p. 12).

The small-scale journeys my interlocutors took me on, connecting seemingly random city spaces, demonstrated their subjectivities. This subjectivity was established through their spatial biographies, where both their movements and narratives created a connection between the city spaces. Their spatial narratives allowed me to move beyond an exclusive emphasis on their experiences of Islamophobia and otherisation. Instead, I explored how experiences and contestations of racism were only one part of their complex life stories. The four cases presented in the following provide an insight into

108 *Muslim Pathways and Spatial Narratives*

the diverse lives of young Montreal Muslims that go beyond the potential stigma and exclusion they might experience from ethnonationalist political discourse. Rather, they emphasise rootedness in the city through family history, personal experiences, and social positioning.

Family History Narrated through a Childhood Neighbourhood

On a cold January morning in Montreal, I met up with 21-year-old Sidra. She was going to take me on a tour of her childhood neighbourhood in southwest Montreal, not far from downtown Montreal. Her family first moved to this neighbourhood after they arrived in Canada from Bangladesh, and they have lived there ever since. Sidra's tour exemplified the lifelong connections one can create with a residential neighbourhood—knowing every corner and crack in the pavement. Her tour was full of personal life details, where she had played hide-and-seek, the apartment where her best friends lived, the good she experienced growing up there, and the stigma that was attributed to the neighbourhood but that she paid no attention to growing up there. As an inner-city area, this southwest neighbourhood had been affected by poverty and crime, and thus for many years there was a social stigma to living in the area. However, the neighbourhood's tainted history was changing during the time of my fieldwork as gentrification efforts were reinvigorating the neighbourhood. Young professionals and students wanting close accommodation to the city centre were moving in, while the poorer working class and communities of colour were being financially pushed out.

When I interviewed her at her university campus a few weeks prior to our walk, Sidra gave me an extensive description of her experiences coming of age in Montreal. She was now going to walk me through these experiences on a tour of her version of Montreal. Sidra's parents immigrated to Canada when her oldest brother was a young child, and they have since lived in the same district in southwest Montreal. This area of Montreal had historically housed many Caribbean and South Asian immigrants, often working class and living in social housing. The population demographics had been rapidly changing over the previous decade. The neighbourhood was experiencing a financial boost through various gentrification schemes: the construction of condos, townhouses, and the proliferation of new commercial enterprises attracted to the area because of its proximity to Montreal's city centre. Sidra had lived in this district since she was born. While her parents had lived in different apartments, they had stayed in the same neighbourhood. Her tour of the area provided an interesting glimpse of the relationship between personal life history and city history. As the district became transformed by gentrification, Sidra and her family experienced social mobility. Her parents' neighbourhood store, which was situated next door to the second of Sidra's childhood rental apartments, was doing well enough for her parents to become houseowners, buying a duplex property in the neighbourhood just before property values significantly rose. This fortunate investment meant that Sidra

Spatial Biographies and Rootedness in Montreal 109

and her three siblings, all university students, could live near their university campuses, and her parents could supplement their income by renting out the spare apartment to university students needing affordable accommodation.

I met Sidra at a metro station in her residential neighbourhood. The first thing she wanted to show me was the community garden where her family had maintained a plot when she was a child. On that cold January morning, it was difficult to picture what the garden looked like under all that snow, but Sidra was there to describe the many summers her parents had spent in that garden (Figure 5.1).

> It's one of those community gardens, so everybody has their own plots. We grew all sorts of things: tomatoes, squash, spinach, chili peppers. They've changed it, they didn't have that fence. We don't actually have a [community] garden [plot] anymore, because we have a big backyard, and my parents grow things there. We had it when we lived in an apartment. It was free. The main supervisor passed away a few months ago, they're all senior citizens. And every year they would have a harvest festival, "The best garden" kind of thing. One of my parents' friends would win every year.
> (Sidra, Montreal)

This first stop on Sidra's city tour represented neighbourhood life for her parents as new immigrants. The community garden was a way for her parents to get to know their neighbours. The fact that the neighbourhood had a

Figure 5.1 Community allotment where Sidra's parents had a plot when they first settled in Montreal.

substantial number of Bangladeshi and other South Asian immigrants meant that the garden became a way to socialise with neighbours without feeling foreign. In this quote, she described how her family stopped needing the communal gardens as they upgraded to their current house, which had a large backyard where her parents grew their vegetables. Meanwhile, the garden supervisor passed away and most of the people she had known who still maintained community garden plots were senior citizens. The physical garden became a relic of her parents' initial integration into Montreal community life. As their social mobility increased, the garden lost its function. Nevertheless, as Sidra narrated, the garden was still an important symbol of her parents' experience of settling down in Montreal. It was a nostalgic reminder of where her family had started and how far they had come since (Figure 5.2).

Figure 5.2 The door to Sidra's first apartment where she and her sister used to practise Bengali writing, Montreal.

Spatial Biographies and Rootedness in Montreal 111

All the kids in the neighbourhood, we were all friends. We used to play hide and seek all around the neighbourhood. There's a little courtyard, where we would play soccer. Our friends would yell from downstairs: "Guys, come down and play". That's all we did, just go out and play.

This is our door and we used to practice Bengali writing on the door with my mom's lipstick. [The door] was green before but now they've renovated it.

Those three windows up there were ours. [It smells like cooking].

It's probably Bengali cooking. It's an immigrant neighbourhood, there's a mixture of everything. This is definitely renovated; it was not like that.

(Sidra, Montreal)

Walking past Sidra's first home, she alternated between reminiscing about her childhood experiences and explaining what had changed since. To a certain extent, this southwestern district was still an immigrant neighbourhood, yet it had been renovated and redeveloped since Sidra's childhood. Like Sidra's family, many of her childhood friends and their families had become more established in Montreal. Those who chose to stay in the neighbourhood after its gentrification were the ones who were financially able to, while others had been forced to move further away from the downtown area (Figure 5.3).

Figure 5.3 Sidra's childhood park, Montreal.

112 *Muslim Pathways and Spatial Narratives*

> So, this is the park, it's my childhood park.
>
> Do you see those green things, there used to be a huge basket swing and all of us kids used to sit there and two other kids would go on the sides and swing. It would go super high.
>
> There used to be a huge slide – well, it's not that huge anymore. We used to hang on these and my aunt used to push us. It's the same slide, same swing-set.
>
> (Sidra, Montreal)

It was important to Sidra to show me her childhood park; this was where she had spent a large portion of her childhood. Whether playing with her aunt, who looked after her, or with the neighbourhood children, this park was an important reminder of her connection to this area. It was a biographical piece of her humble beginnings growing up in an inner-city neighbourhood. While there were many social problems in the area, the way Sidra reminisced about her childhood experiences was mainly positive.

Although many families that lived in the area were struggling financially when Sidra was a child, she and the other neighbourhood children seemed to make the most of their circumstances. The benefits of living in a neighbourhood that had so many young families, outweighed the hardships and uncertainties faced by their parents who often were struggling as newly arrived immigrants (Figure 5.4).

Figure 5.4 Inside Sidra's family store, Montreal.

Spatial Biographies and Rootedness in Montreal 113

The next stop on Sidra's tour was a brief visit to her family's shop:

> And that's our store. It's a very residential neighbourhood. Downtown is just up the tunnel, Concordia is right there. [We walk inside the store, we greet Sidra's mom and her friend] This is mostly an African neighbourhood, so we sell things we've never heard of, like plantain, we love their plantain, we got those for them. And this, they call it Malanga, so there's a lot of new foods I've discovered. We've got our Arab grape leaves. And there's a lot of Bengalis around here as well, so we have our Bengali chutney. [We look around the store] The house we used to live in is right next door.
>
> (Sidra, Montreal)

With every stop along the tour, the narrative arc of Sidra's spatial biography became clearer. Her relationship not just with her neighbourhood, but with the larger city was rooted in every memory she had of her past. The city and car noises that might be viewed as bothersome by many people were for Sidra a happy reminder of growing up right in front of a busy highway. As such, Sidra concluded, "I was born in the city."

The next stop on Sidra's tour was the local mosque she and her sister used to go when they were growing up (Figure 5.5).

Figure 5.5 Sidra's local mosque, Montreal.

114   *Muslim Pathways and Spatial Narratives*

> We're headed to [X-mosque] now.
>
> [Greets someone] It's nice coming here [the street she used to live in] because I see them [old neighbours], and they recognize me.
>
> This is [X]-mosque. The front entrance we use when we have halaqah [Islamic study circle].
>
> (Sidra, Montreal)

As we approached the metro station to travel to the mosque, Sidra greeted an acquaintance on the way. It happened several times during Sidra's tour that she greeted people on the street—young and old and of different ethnicities. It gave me a sense that I was on her turf. This neighbourhood that stretched over three metro stations was in fact *her city*. The neighbourhood included representations of her ethnic heritage and religious identification, but also all the cultural artefacts and foods that she and her family had adopted as a result of owning a store in a culturally diverse neighbourhood. There was a conviviality about her spatial account. In many ways, Sidra's account is defined by a convivial life of her childhood neighbourhood. This conviviality glosses over the challenges of structural racism and ethnonationalist political discourse existing in the wider society. Instead, it celebrates the local solidarity expressed through communal engagements across differences.

This southwestern district gave Sidra the possibility of rooting and developing herself within the neighbourhood, allowing all her intersecting identifications to meet and integrate seamlessly.

We left the mosque and headed for our final stop on Sidra's tour: her current family home (Figure 5.6).

> As you can see the distance from the metro to our house is much further away than before. One of the buses in front of the house takes us straight to [my university] and another bus goes to [another university], where my brother goes. [...]My parents when they were looking for a place, they found a bunch of cheaper places in the suburbs, but they were thinking of us and how we would have to commute. [Sidra greets a neighbor, explaining:] He's kinda *the* neighbourhood, the person everyone knows. He just moved in, in the summer and he's a carpenter, I introduced myself to them. I've always liked that everybody is super close [in the neighbourhood].
>
> (Sidra, Montreal)

Ending our tour in her family home epitomised the social mobility she and her family had experienced within the same neighbourhood. When viewing her first family home at the beginning of our tour, Sidra highlighted how the apartment building had been renovated and looked different than its appearance when she was a child, when the neighbourhood was economically neglected. Her current family home looks newly renovated and depicts a new version of this urban quarter. It represents a settled middle-class family

Figure 5.6 Sidra's current home, Montreal.

with grown children that are finishing higher degrees—the epitome of social mobility. Many struggling families in this district have been pushed further out to the periphery of the city because of gentrification schemes that have increased rental prices. Sidra's parents were able to make a fortunate investment that ultimately allowed them to sustain the roots they had planted in this area. As we left her family home and headed towards the metro, her final comment as she greeted the neighbourhood carpenter was telling of her connection to the neighbourhood. She enjoyed feeling a sense of closeness with her neighbours, even with the many changes that the district had experienced in recent years. Her personal biography was connected to the neighbourhood, so much so that she took it upon herself to introduce herself to new neighbours, as if inviting them into *her* neighbourhood.

A Seasonal Walk through a Multicultural Neighbourhood

The following case introduces a very different story of settlement and rootedness. It emphasises the spatial narrative of Amy, who was an aspiring and very talented artist. At the time of our interview and walk tour, she had recently graduated with an art degree and was completing her postgraduate school applications to several prestigious university art departments. She is of Anglo-European descent and grew up in a small town in Ontario. She was introduced to Islam by her non-Muslim high school ethics teacher not long after 9/11, and some years later, at the age of 17, she decided to convert to Islam. At the time of our walk, she had been Muslim for several years, and so her Muslimness and spirituality were seamlessly woven into her narrative.

Amy started her tour from her apartment in a western district of Montreal on a freezing but sunny December day. In minus 20 degrees Celsius, we left her cosy studio apartment and walked down the residential street of duplex houses and apartments. I gave Amy the camera to allow her to control what to take pictures of. Amy's artistic gaze coloured most of her being-in-the-city. She was excited to take me on a tour of her favourite area: Côte-des-Neiges (CDN), just a short walk from where she lived. This was a walk she often took when needing artistic inspiration. Looking up to notice her surroundings, she urged me to notice things around us which I normally would not have paid attention to (Figure 5.7).

Figure 5.7 Balcony observed on Amy's walk, where she speaks about looking up when having an artistic bloc, Côte-des-Neiges, Montreal.

Spatial Biographies and Rootedness in Montreal 117

We'll walk to Côte-des-Neiges and you'll see my [city]. One of my professors was telling me if you have an artistic block, and you keep hitting that wall and you can't figure out how to get through it. She gave us a list that I thought was kinda a stupid thing to do to try to get you out of your habit. The best thing ever that worked for me, it probably makes me look like an idiot, is: look up. You know how many things I've noticed just by looking up.

There's so much emphasis on eye-level. When you look up, you start seeing things like this guy over here has the coolest patio, I see it all the time, I'll take a picture of it. The detail on the rod iron, I love it. And you start seeing the differences between things. [...] Sometimes you'll see cats and dogs just staring at you. I've always lived on this side of the city. It's great, close to downtown, close to everything. I love this place, it's very quiet. The older I get the more I like quiet.

Downtown you'll notice little bird trees if you look up. That's actually where a lot of my inspiration comes from, even in my artwork, comes from looking up. Even if you wanna talk spiritually. It reminds me that this little microcosm of my life that makes me freak out, there's something so much bigger than me. It puts things into perspective.

(Amy, Montreal)

As we walked down the street she lived on, Amy described how important her neighbourhood was to her. She had lived in Montreal ever since she started her undergraduate degree four years prior, and during that time, Montreal had become what she associated with home. The small Ontario town she was born and raised in had become too confining for her to express herself. For Amy, the neighbourhood she now lived in allowed her to be close to urban life yet feel the solitude and quiet of suburbia. This was evident as we walked down her street on a weekday morning—no cars or noise to be heard. She explained how her routinised walk towards Côte-des-Neiges (CDN) street was often an inspirational experience, as she tried to become unhabituated to her environment by looking up over her eye level (Figure 5.8).

This is my normal route if I want to go to CDN [the main street in the area]. I would go without a purpose. I'll show you, I have an obsession with Saint Joseph Oratory. I've gone in a couple of times. On my Instagram, I have this documented, changes of weather of [the] Oratory, and I just love it. I've found it when it's foggy, covered in snow. It's quiet. Even as a Muslim. I was raised Christian, right, even some of those notions I have of prayer and sanctity is not against Islam. It's something I let myself engage in even though it might not be a direct part. For me it's the only symbol I have in Montreal of that feeling of greater importance than just this daily status quo of people just running around chaotic. I'll take a picture of it from my favourite spot. Do you see the windows around the bottom of the dome, they light up at night, and they're like gold.

(Amy, Montreal)

Figure 5.8 Saint Joseph's Oratory observed during Amy's walk, Côte-des-Neiges, Montreal.

As we walked down the main street taking us to a large intersection, Amy took a picture of St. Joseph Oratory in the distance. The Oratory is a hallmark of Montreal's skyline and a major tourist attraction. For Amy, however, it was a spiritual reminder. She was raised Christian, and although she was now Muslim, she still associated the Oratory with a sense of spirituality. The Oratory became a reminder of something more profound than the hustle and bustle of urban life. It was even a reminder of the changing seasons and thus the changing times. Amy kept noticing the Oratory in the distance throughout our walk, taking pictures of it from different angles. With these continuous reminders, she made sure I understood its significance. The Oratory was a public reminder of spirituality for her. She did not have to go

Spatial Biographies and Rootedness in Montreal 119

to a mosque or remove herself from the world; she simply had to look up to the horizon and she would be reminded of a greater sense of existence.

> This is a corner I spend a lot of my life at, because I either get off the bus here and I go down here and wait for the 165 to go downtown. Or this is where my meandering begins if you can call it that. This connects me to everything, I do groceries that way, I have friends who live that way, this goes to the [sufi]- center, the spiritual center [mosque] I go to. Obviously, home is this way, and school is that way. So, it's kinda my four corners. I like it at night because of the Christmas lights.
>
> (Amy, Montreal)

Not everything posed as much spiritual and artistic symbolism for Amy as the Oratory. Some places were just avenues to reach other destinations, such as the intersection depicted in Figure 5.9. The intersection linked four roads that connected her to various parts of the city; one street took her to her favourite shops and restaurants, the area in which she socialised with friends as well as in which she found solitude in the crowd. This was the area that she wanted to show me in particular. Another street took her to the mosque she preferred to frequent, while yet another street connected her to downtown Montreal, where she went to university. And finally, one street led her home to her cosy studio apartment.

On the CDN high street, we stop at a bookshop Amy often goes to. She shares her experiences of wandering through the store (Figure 5.10).

> I get a lot of inspiration walking around looking at stuff because I get to control the input than just walking down the street where there's a flow of input going in everywhere. There's a lot of stuff around, but it's more that I've gone to a place to zen out.
>
> (Amy, Montreal)

The bookshop Amy took me to was a large franchise bookshop with mostly French books and other eclectic and decorative items. While Amy did speak French, it was not her first language, but she explained that the store was a place of inspiration found in the random and unique items it carried. She pointed out that in the store, she could control what drew her attention as opposed to walking down the street where there was a continuous stream of inputs beyond her control. Throughout her tour, Amy narrated this juxtaposition between the love she had for living in a city environment and often finding it overstimulating. To relieve this tension, she sought places like the bookshop or little parks and markets that sheltered her from the chaotic feel of the city (Figure 5.11).

> Let's do the park, but there's not much to see there because it's covered in snow. It's a place I go in the summertime, because I would just lay and just veg, read a book, where I would leave my phone at

120 *Muslim Pathways and Spatial Narratives*

Figure 5.9 Intersection connecting Amy to her different city spaces, Côte-des-Neiges, Montreal.

home and just sleep. It's very important for me to disconnect. It's becoming unconnected from here and becoming connected to something else. Tapping into this kind of ... I was given a glimpse into spiritual and creative potential and I realize if I want to attain that, I have to work at it. I guess for me, one of the things is that feeling unmediated in order to mediate myself is maybe the optimum for myself.

(Amy, Montreal)

Figure 5.10 Display table in the bookshop Amy enjoys visiting, Côte-des-Neiges, Montreal.

Behind the busy high street of Côte-des-Neiges, Amy took me to one of the parks she would go to during the summer, explaining the differences between the seasons where in the winter there was a hockey rink, which in the summer was a large grass field. With every stop on the tour, Amy constructed meaning through her narrative; the Oratory, the intersection, and the bookshop were all given personal significance and meaning through her narration. The park was no different, and Amy explained that this place was where she came to disconnect from her phone, from people, and from social demands and reconnect with herself. While she was explaining her need to

122 *Muslim Pathways and Spatial Narratives*

Figure 5.11 The park where Amy goes to relax and disconnect in the summertime, Côte-des-Neiges, Montreal.

feel unmediated, her phone vibrated and she exclaimed: "That's it – people can basically get a hold of you on text, Facebook, Messenger and Instagram. You can literally be at someone's beck and call at all times if you let them." This notion of always having to be accessible to people seemed to be a disruption to Amy, as if she had to stop her train of thought to engage with people through various social media outlets. Amy's attempt to find solitude in the park, where she could be anonymous in the crowd, was challenged by her phone—a virtual space that connected her with her social network even when she tried to escape it.

The final stop on Amy's tour was a small independent café on a side street to CDN (Figure 5.12). Inside the café there was a distinctive urban aesthetic interior design with vintage sofas and rustic wood tables and modern political art on the walls, combining feelings of a quaint old-fashioned living room with a modern urban feel to it. We ended our tour with a cup of tea and a long talk about where she was headed in life. Amy was planning to leave Canada to live abroad for a few months while waiting to hear back about her application to postgraduate degrees in Europe. She was excited about exploring her opportunities outside of Montreal; she had already lived abroad during an internship programme and was excited about the prospects of travelling again and potentially living in Europe while doing her graduate studies.

Spatial Biographies and Rootedness in Montreal 123

Figure 5.12 Inside the café Amy took me to in Côte-des-Neiges, Montreal.

My conversations and tour with Amy exemplify how personal connections to—and use of—city spaces can become deeply rooted over a relatively short period of time through a process of habituation. As Amy pointed out things of significance to her, she continued to highlight how these places changed in function and importance to her during different times of the year. Contrary to Sidra, Amy had only moved to Montreal as a young university student. As such, she did not share the lifelong history in the city that Sidra had. So, while Sidra could take me on a life narrative through her childhood neighbourhood, Amy allowed me to appreciate the process through which someone *creates* ties to a locality. It is through the habitual use of space and allowing oneself to create meaning and add personal importance to that space that one adopts a locality as one's own. Amy took me to spaces that she had grown accustomed to by walking and using them throughout her years in Montreal. However, she was at a crossroads in her life when she took me on her tour. She was about to move to a new city and hopefully develop new connections to its spaces.

What Amy's tour exemplifies is the fact that being rooted in a locality is something that is developed not only through lifelong connections but may also become significant over a shorter period of time through one's use of the spaces in everyday life. Rootedness is thus established through the process of habituation when city spaces go from being new and unfamiliar to being familiar and personally connected to a part of one's life history.

Planting Roots in a Suburban Immigrant Neighbourhood

This next spatial narrative focuses on Adam's walk tour, a young man whom I briefly introduced in Chapter 1. Adam had a mixed Iranian and Armenian background and was also a Muslim convert. He took me on a short walk through the suburban neighbourhood he and his family had first lived in when they immigrated to Canada. This was an immigrant neighbourhood located in the West Island of Montreal, a suburban area. Unlike Sidra or Amy's neighbourhoods, the immigrants living in this West Island district were mostly middle-class professionals, temporarily living in rental apartments until they could save enough capital to buy a property.

Adam's tour was not about the interaction between urban restructuring and social mobility as in Sidra's case. Rather, Adam depicted the opportunities that were available to immigrants who had educational and social capital *prior* to immigration. These immigrants had an easier pathway towards establishing a foothold, financially, professionally, and socially, in their new country. The upper middle-class position of Adam's family prior to migration made it easier to establish themselves in Montreal. Whether in his mother's church, in the neighbourhood he grew up in, or even as a Muslim convert, Adam seemed to have been well-rooted in a Montreal middle-class category throughout.

Adam's family migrated to Canada when he was 7 years old, and the main area of his tour traversed the neighbourhood where he lived from his early time in Canada until he completed high school (Figure 5.13).

Figure 5.13 The townhouse where Adam first lived when his family migrated to Canada. West Island, Montreal.

Spatial Biographies and Rootedness in Montreal 125

This is where I used to live for a few years, most of high school. It's like a townhouse. It's a complex of buildings, and in the back, you have an open space where they have a pool and a field and that's where we used to play a lot as kids. My summers, we would just spend outside playing tag, guns, soccer, sports. That's where I spent my time as a kid.

It's kind of a ghettoish neighbourhood, you had a lot of kids doing drugs, smoking and stuff like that. Now that I think about it, I kind of consider it a minor miracle that I never fell into this kind of thing. [...] It's not so much disadvantaged, it's kind of a halfway community. A lot of immigrants come here before they move on to more suburban areas. [...] In any area where there's a lot of young people and not a lot of parental supervision, kids do whatever they want.

(Adam, Montreal)

The neighbourhood Adam showed me was located behind a major road in West Island. The West Island is an area of Montreal that is usually associated with middle and upper-class families who often speak more English than French. As we walked closer to the small townhouses clustered together, Adam pointed out his old childhood home. As he explained in the above quote, this neighbourhood was more likely to house struggling residents than other areas of the West Island.

The neighbourhood attracted working-class families looking for affordable housing, but it also attracted immigrants who, while living in the neighbourhood, could look forward to better job and career prospects. This would allow them move on to bigger and more permanent homes in more affluent neighbourhoods. Adam was conscious of the class-based differences between himself and his childhood friends. Reflecting back on his years in this neighbourhood, Adam explained that it was not necessarily the most disadvantaged neighbourhood. Nevertheless, some of the neighbourhood youth did struggle with alcohol and drug abuse.

Most of the immigrants I knew who lived here, came in, stayed a few years and then moved out into a house or further away. I think I lived here for maybe 5 years.

(Adam, Montreal)

Like other immigrant families, Adam's family lived in the neighbourhood for a few years before they were able to afford buying a nice house further away from the busy main street. However, Adam described how the move to a more upscale suburban area resulted in a sense of unfamiliarity. Neighbours did not know each other like in the close-knit neighbourhood that was his first Canadian home. Comparing the two neighbourhoods, Adam seemed nostalgic about his childhood home. Despite some of its negative traits, he had enjoyed being surrounded by other young children when living there. Adam described his experiences growing up in this area as carefree; he spent

126 *Muslim Pathways and Spatial Narratives*

Figure 5.14 The fence where Adam played with the neighbourhood kids, West Island, Montreal.

most of his time playing in the park that was reserved for the residents of the townhouses. The only struggle he related was the make-believe feud between the kids in his block and the neighbouring block (Figure 5.14).

> And we would have fights ... So, there's a fence there and we would have beefs with the people from across the fence, they were known as "the across the fence" people. Just childish stuff like that. And then there was also "the across the street" people, but then we kinda got along with them. Just fun child times. There used to be a hole that made it easier to go from one neighbourhood to another and we would always close it because we can't have a hole with 'the across the fence' people. So, when people [adults] found it, they would be like "Why the hell are you blocking this hole, what is wrong with you kids?!". There was no difference in the social class or anything between us.
>
> (Adam, Montreal)

Although they seemed aware of their different ethnic and social backgrounds, Adam and his friends were connected by the fact that they lived in close proximity to each other and were around the same age. This meant that Adam did not have to go far to find friends, but the dependence on residential

Spatial Biographies and Rootedness in Montreal 127

proximity also meant that these were the friends he lost contact with soon after he left the neighbourhood.

In many ways, Adam's tour focused on his nostalgic memories of childhood, where friendships were developed based on being on the right side of the communal fence. However, as he grew older, his family moved and, more importantly Adam's circumstances changed. Adam became more focused on his school as opposed to his neighbourhood friends, who did not plan on continuing onto higher education. They did not share his love for video gaming either, and he did not share their association of fun with drinking alcohol. So, Adam and his childhood friends drifted apart. What remained, however, was the nostalgic sentiment of coming of age together in a neighbourhood where working-class white Montrealers lived side-by-side with middle-class immigrants trying to realise social mobility. Adam's narrative highlights how migration often leads to downward social mobility. Often, migrants, especially if they enjoyed a higher socioeconomic status in their countries of origin, struggle to gain social mobility or even sustain a similar status in their destination. Adam and his family's migration experiences were not much different. They left Iran, where they had enjoyed an upper-class lifestyle, and settled in Canada, where initially they were a part of a lower-middle-class community. However, it wasn't long before they gained social mobility, as his parents were able to transfer their professional positions to Canada.

Rootedness through Family Connections with a Religious Community

The final Montreal narrative depicts Yaqub's tour. His family had lived in Montreal for almost three generations. His maternal grandfather had come to Montreal in the 1960s and his mother had therefore attended high school and university in the city. His father had also lived in Montreal for many years and had started a successful business. His tour exemplified how spatial rootedness can be affected by family history, and how this history frames a sense of connection to the city.

Yaqub's tour was different from other tours I had been on in Montreal because we had to drive rather than walk to many of his destinations. He had lived most of his life in the West Island suburb of Montreal, so Yaqub was accustomed to driving or taking the bus to different places, whether for school or social activities. The first stop on his tour was the main mall in the West Island (Figure 5.15).

> This is Fairview mall, it was basically my whole high school career, I guess. Me and my friends, whenever we would meet up, we would always come here. We used to go to the mall a lot, walk around, chill out here.
>
> (Yaqub, Montreal)

128 *Muslim Pathways and Spatial Narratives*

Figure 5.15 Bus Station at the local mall. This is where Yaqub would take the bus to school and come to hang out at the mall. West Island, Montreal.

Yaqub would spend a lot of his spare time in the mall socialising with friends during his high school years. The idea of hanging out and socialising in the mall is typical for North American suburban youth. Because of the city infrastructure and the way North American suburbs were initially constructed, the mall became one of the main places suburban youth go to socialise. The mall was also the point of departure if Yaqub needed to go anywhere. This is where the main bus terminal was located, providing him with transportation to school, home, or any other place.

> This is my old house, I was brought up here for the majority of my life. All of my teen years pretty much. A lot of experiences here, my brother was born here. We used to have the halaqah [religious study circle] in here, in the basement. We used to have two basketball nets. Our neighbors were Muslims as well, so they had a basketball net and we had one, and we set up … When we were kids, we would play basketball after the halaqah on the streets in the driveway.
>
> If you can see all of those dents, those are from me when I used to play hockey.
>
> […]A lot of memories here, good times. We had a lot of activities here. My friends would come hang out until late at night. We used to have the *halaqah* [Islamic study circle] here. A lot of Muslim events,

Figure 5.16 Yaqub's childhood home where he lived most of his child- and youthhood. West Island, Montreal.

gatherings and stuff, like our current house. We used to do food basket in the garage, the Ramadan food basket. [Our house] has always been very active, this house and our new house as well.

Alhamdulillah [praise be to God], people were always coming and we're very familiar with the Muslim community at large.

(Yaqub, Montreal)

This stop on Yaqub's tour was his childhood home and street (Figures 5.16 and 5.17). He narrated his childhood memories of the place, explaining how the street looked different when he lived there, with fewer houses and more green areas. He figuratively transformed the house and street through his narrative, taking me 10 years back to when he used to live there. He highlighted the few things that physically remained, like the dents on the carport from when he used to play hockey. Other things, such as the hedge and the new houses, had been transformed to the point where they had no connection to his memories of the street. It was clear that the physical signs of his memories were slowly disappearing through the changes the new house owners had made to his childhood home. Even on this suburban street, the physical transformation was evident. Nevertheless, I sensed the nostalgia Yaqub was transmitting through his narrative, describing how the space looked when he was a child, and how the difference in layout allowed for a different use of the space.

130 *Muslim Pathways and Spatial Narratives*

Figure 5.17 Dents in the carports, which are from Yaqub when he used to play hockey. West Island, Montreal.

> This was like one of the first non-desi halal places that we used to go to. So, when we used to go to the older halaqah, by that time I was 15-16 until almost 20, for like 4-5-6 years, this is the place we used to always go to after halaqah. Literally, for 5-6 years straight. This was where I was first introduced to Arab food, we loved it. Now I feel bad we don't come here anymore, very rarely. Now there are other alternatives.
> (Yaqub, Montreal)

After visiting his childhood home, Yaqub took me to the Falafel restaurant that had been his favourite when he was younger (Figure 5.18). The place is not as popular among his friends anymore. With the change of demographics and more Muslim restaurant entrepreneurs in the West Island, there were many other halal and vegetarian options, reducing the Falafel restaurant to a nostalgic souvenir of Yaqub's youth.

> So, this is [X] *masjid* [mosque]. Obviously initially it wasn't like this, it used to be a house. It was expanded around 8 years ago, so it was a house before. Obviously, that was more homey, that was mainly where I was brought up and I can more relate to. It was like *my masjid*. We used to spend all of our time there, especially in Ramadan.

Figure 5.18 The local Falafel restaurant where Yaqub would go to eat after religious study circles (*halaqah*).

So, a good portion of my Islamic life was spent here. It was the families that would come with kids around the same age. For us, we're all older now, so it's not the same. But it was fun, it was like ... this was our community gathering, this was the hub when we were younger. For me, now it's not as much, we're doing so many different things. When you're younger, you just do whatever your parents tell you to do, come here, and, like, everyone is in a similar stage in life. Now everyone is in different stages of life, some people are graduating, kids, different countries, cities. The *iftars*, the old-timers don't come anymore, now it's more the young families, so there's definitely more of a disconnect now.

(Yaqub, Montreal)

This last place Yaqub wanted to show me was the mosque he had been attending throughout his life (Figure 5.19). He described how the physical building itself had changed dramatically since he was a child. With that change, he had also lost some of the sense of rootedness that he associated with the old building. It was in that building where his childhood memories of playing and enjoying the community events were formed. Yaqub provided a detailed narrative of why this mosque was so important to him. He described the

Figure 5.19 The local mosque where Yaqub used to come as a child. West Island, Montreal.

childhood fun he used to have with other young kids attending the mosque with their families. Yaqub was eager to narrate the fond memories he connected with this particular mosque. It was because of these memories that he would continue to prefer this mosque over others in the area. However, for Yaqub, as well as many other young Muslims I met, the mosque was not necessarily the place they felt most connected to. Rather, the Muslim Student Associations as well as informal social networks, where friends would meet on a weekly basis to study and discuss religious topics, were more important to many of them.

Yaqub's tour depicted the long multi-generational connection he and his family had established in Montreal since his grandfather immigrated in the 1960s. Because of his long family history in the city, spanning three generations, Yaqub grew up in a stable middle-class environment. His spatial narrative presents a different sort of city connection, one that spans beyond his years to include the experiences of his parents and grandparents.

Conclusion

This chapter explored what happened when I stopped asking my Montreal participants about their Muslimness and experiences of racism and started

Spatial Biographies and Rootedness in Montreal 133

asking them about their city. They were empowered to decide what was important. They showed me childhood homes, stores, parks, neighbourhoods, and mosques. Through these tours, Montreal was represented in a multitude of spaces that had personal significance to the young Muslims' lives. In these representations, Montreal was not *one* city designed by urban planners, investors, and construction contractors. Rather, the city was comprised of a wide range of distinct and differently experienced city-spaces. The young Muslims I met personalised these spaces by weaving them into their life stories. As their narratives were rooted in the city, these youth also became witnesses to the city's history.

This history had a direct impact on the physical preservation of my participants' memories. The top-down restructuring of city spaces was not concerned about Sidra's fond memories of the green door of her first childhood home in southwestern Montreal, where she and her sister marked their belonging by practising their Bengali writing on the doorway. Yet, Sidra's memories remained and became a testimony for what used to be and what has taken its place since. The notion that our nostalgia is connected to a space set in a particular time is one of the most valuable insights of the tours I conducted in Montreal. We remember and narrate our stories as they were set and experienced in the past, regardless of how the physical space has changed since. However, as my participants took me to visit these sites of their core memories, they looked for what remained and what had changed. Finding a lasting sign from one's childhood, like the dents in Yaqub's old carport, validated one's narrative. Likewise, noticing the changes, and reminiscing about how it used to be, highlights the nostalgia connected to a particular time and space that can only be reminisced about but never recreated.

6 Space, Time, and the Urban Muslim

Some time after I concluded my fieldwork, a Montreal participant and friend, Lisa, asked me about the progress of my research. She was especially interested in hearing the "results" of the spatial tours I had been conducting; a part of my research she found fascinating from the start.

Apologetic about the slowness of my research progress, I shared with her some of my initial thoughts and my uncertainty about what direction I should take in employing this ethnographic material. Instead of leading the conversation, I tried to make room for her to share her interest in my research. Lisa was a third-year English literature major with a love for culturally diverse and socially critical literature. In one of her literature classes, they had been discussing the Australian aboriginal practice of "walkabout" as a rite of passage. Lisa was reminded of the city tour she had taken me on when she read the literature describing the aboriginal significance of "walkabout." For her, her tour represented a sort of "walkabout" that she had been doing throughout her life that she had invited me into. Lisa took me on a walk around Old Pointe Claire Village in the West Island of Montreal. We walked through this village as she had done countless times throughout her childhood and youth, usually aimlessly. Through her narrative, this aimless "walkabout" was instilled with importance as a spatial representation of her life narrative. It was through this kind of narrative process that was employed by the young people I met that the significance of their movements was demonstrated. These movements were biographical, subjective, *and* social.

This chapter provides a comparative conclusion to the ethnographic material presented in Chapters 4 and 5, highlighting the theoretical significance of the urban "walkabouts" my participants took me on. It demonstrates how spatial accounts can provide rich ethnographic windows onto life stories and self-representation. These urban "walkabouts" may be very different from the nomadic lifestyle that characterises the traditional walkabout. Nonetheless, they highlight the importance of routinised and localised mobilities. The pathways we use on a regular basis become instilled with both biographical and representational importance. Whether the walks I was taken on demonstrated personal history, self-representation, or both, they were significant factors in demonstrating the pathways crafted by young Muslims through the localities in which they resided. Such pathways created

DOI: 10.4324/9781003294696-9

Space, Time, and the Urban Muslim   135

lingering connections to their being-in-the-city. City spaces exist irrespective of our use of them; however, the unique pathways that we create as we walk, drive, or bike through the spaces create a relationship between us and those spaces. It is the pathways that are the connecting factor between social actors and physical spaces. Spaces are thus attributed personal meaning and become proof of our life pathways and/or representations of our identifications, social mobility, and future potentials.

I start this chapter by placing my ethnographic material within a wider theoretical background focused on mobility and movement. I initially decided to use spatial tours as an ethnographic method, building on a larger theoretical legacy of migration studies and more contemporary approaches to mobility and movement theory within social and cultural research. In Chapters 4 and 5, I sought to develop an appreciation of pathways and the choices young Muslims made in selecting certain spaces as part of their tours rather than others, both biographically and socially. In this concluding chapter, I bring together the ethnographic materials presented in the previous two chapters, drawing comparisons between my Montreal and Copenhagen interlocutors. The aim of this chapter is thus to depict the value of comparative ethnography, as it brings our attention to the local, sociopolitical, and global similarities and differences that would otherwise go unnoticed.

Theorising Mobility and Urban Pathways

In his book *Mobilities* (2007), John Urry argues for an approach to understanding mobility as a paradigm. He seeks to divert our attention away from social structures and order towards a paradigmatic focus on mobility. Urry expands the definition of mobility to include widely disparate phenomena: corporal travel, physical movement of objects, imaginative travel, virtual travel, communicative travel, as well as social mobility and movements of ideas and concepts. This multi-stranded concept of mobility is useful to think with when engaging with young Muslims in Montreal and Copenhagen, who used the spatial tours to demonstrate both their physical and social mobility. Firstly, their movements within city spaces demonstrated their ability to understand and navigate urban spatialisation. For instance, they chose to go to one neighbourhood for its positive social connotations, while dismissing a nearby neighbourhood for its stigmatised associations. Secondly, their spatial mobility was a representation of time, depicting past experiences and connections to localities or describing future aspirations and expectations through their movements. Thirdly, these young people represented their own social mobility through their spatial narratives, from growing up in an inner-city neighbourhood to becoming successful university students.

> Spatial biography foregrounds the spaces that condense the movements connecting and constituting them: the telling of a life through its scenes of enactment and co-composition, a here, and then a there,

136 *Muslim Pathways and Spatial Narratives*

weaving time flexibly through the prism of memory, and the reconfig-
ured modalities of space, as personal stories.

(Amit & Knowles, 2017, p. 12)

Spatial biography thus becomes an enactment of personal history through movement. It allows for a different life story to be told, one that is grounded in a physical space as well as memory. Some of my participants chose to construct a spatial
account that created a spatial biography. For instance, Sidra took me from one
space to another, connecting the spaces through her memories, noting the change
of the space or sometimes the lack of change. Her spatial biography ended in
her present family home. This family home became a strong symbol of her and
her family's social mobility without her explicitly narrating this change in social
position. This was only possible since the preceding spatial account allowed for a
comparison between the spaces of her past and the spaces of her present.

According to Ruth Finnegan (1989), the concept of pathways illustrates the
relative and situational character of urban life both in social and geographical terms—where people choose to follow certain directions instead of others
(Amit-Talai, 1994; Finnegan, 1989). Based on her study of local musicians
in an English town, Finnegan defines pathways as "a series of known and
regular routes which people chose—or were led into—and which they both
kept open and extended through their actions" (Finnegan, 1989, p. 305). In
other words, we all choose to follow certain paths, both in a physical and a
social sense, and the pathways we choose at any given moment influence our
practices and social relations. Vered Amit further develops this concept in her
study of young people's urban pathways, focusing on how young people in
Montreal and the Outaouais tactically use space, time, and social roles "to
organize their involvements and relationships in the city" (Amit-Talai, 1994,
p. 188). This idea of pathways complements the concept of spatial narratives
in the ethnographic accounts I have presented in Chapter 4 and 5. My use of
pathways is not necessarily focused on planned and structured paths through
city spaces in one's daily life. Rather, pathways demonstrate young Muslims'
knowledge of their city. Some gave me a spatial narrative of their life stories, others wanted to focus on spaces that represented their lifestyle and
social position. Incorporating the idea of pathways into my study of young
Muslims challenges the homogenous understanding of "the Muslim community" as an overarching category of people who share similar lifestyles
and beliefs. Instead, it allows for the diverse and indeterminate ways young
Muslims choose, change, and create social and spatial pathways.

My participants had free reign to show me spaces that were meaningful to them. They ended up constructing pathways that involved a dialectic
between time and space, depicting past, present, and sometimes future use of
urban spaces and what these meant to them. The concept of pathways thus
allows for the processual way in which young Muslims choose, change, and
recreate social and localised pathways. Hence, an important component of
pathways is the idea that they

Space, Time, and the Urban Muslim 137

are relative only and, despite their continuity over time, changing rather than absolute – unlike the picture conveyed by the more concrete-sounding and bounded concepts of "world" or "community."

(Finnegan, 1989, p. 323)

Allowing my interlocutors to construct and enact their unique pathways enabled me to go beyond exploring them as a social group and instead look at young people who share similar social identifications (Muslim, young, urbanite) but enact these in unique and personalised ways. These spatial accounts thus allowed me to explore the social and spatial lives (past, present, and future) of young Muslims, not as a community, but as individuals who are influenced by personal experiences and relations.

All the tours on which my participants took me included institutions (schools, mosques, clubs), personal spaces (homes), and public spaces (streets, parks, cafés, shops). These were not necessarily redefined into "Muslim places," but they enabled an appreciation of my interlocutors' personal attachments to and social positions in their city spaces. The benefit of opening the space of narration to include anything of importance to my interlocutors highlights how these young people were embedded within the spatial fabric of their cities. They navigated the space with an awareness of the social connotations and histories of particular localities.

The Tactics of Spatial Narratives

Michel de Certeau's (2005 [1984]) emphasis on everyday life beyond ideas of domination and resistance is essential for understanding young Muslims' experiences in a nuanced way beyond the Islamophobic rhetoric that exists in public and political debates. Many of my participants responded to such rhetoric with social actions and protest. Yet this was only one part of a much more complex and less eventful regime of everyday life. My Montreal-based fieldwork coincided with political campaigns to ban religious symbols (the Charter of Values). Although several of my participants, particularly the young women, were engaged in resisting these political ploys of domination, when it came to how they saw themselves and their position in this urban context, they emphasised other aspects of their lives. There was no equally heightened political controversy in Denmark at the time of my fieldwork. Nevertheless, there was a similar tendency among my interlocutors to underplay overt resistance in depictions of their daily movements. In both contexts, young Muslims did not represent their everyday lives or movements through the city within a narrative of resistance. Rather, their pathways were constructed by means of ongoing daily negotiations and manoeuvring within urban space, and not in the extraordinary moments of social action.

By concentrating on the uses of space, de Certeau illustrates how imposed structures can become reliable. Thereby, they enable the individual to develop tactics to manipulate these structures. In de Certeau's own words, "making it

138 *Muslim Pathways and Spatial Narratives*

possible to live in them by reintroducing into them the plural mobility of goals and desires" (de Certeau, 2005, p. xxii). De Certeau distinguishes between strategy and tactics to demonstrate an important difference between an ordinary individual's manoeuvring within such structures, and the more powerful strategists who are able to transform them. He thus defines strategy as the ability to manipulate power relations within a specific space (de Certeau, 2005, p. 30). On the other hand, tactics can only make use of and manipulate such spaces through "a degree of plurality and creativity" within confining structures (de Certeau, 2005, p. 30). As "an art of the weak," tactics are the creative responses of non-powerful actors in moments of conjunctures within an imposed structural terrain of hegemonic power (de Certeau: 37).

Young Muslims in Copenhagen and Montreal demonstrated their tactical abilities through their spatial accounts. They used these tactics in their everyday routines without making them explicit. The tactics, however, were nonetheless revealed through the movements and narratives expressed during their tours. For instance, Khadija's choice of avoiding parts of Nørrebro and instead focusing on downtown Copenhagen highlighted her ability to navigate the social connotations that were entrenched in these city spaces. Some spaces represented lower socioeconomic status while other spaces represented affluence. Khadija's choices of the spaces to include in her account demonstrated her acute awareness of her own self-representation through these city structures. This is where her tactical skills became important. They provided her with an ability to represent her quest for social mobility within urban spaces over which she had little power. In other words, the concept of everyday tactics allows an appreciation of how people, such as Khadija, construct creative attempts to manipulate the hidden potentials within urban spaces to claim their social position within these spaces.

As demonstrated by Khadija's narrative, de Certeau emphasises how a person is not only subjected to structures, but can, in fact, enact their agency through such structures as well. He explains how city planners, government officials, and other powerful people develop the structure of the city. They have the privileged position to produce the city structures from above by deciding what buildings to construct and how to pave the roads, etc. However, from the perspective of the individual, these overarching structures are less determinative of an individual's pathways through the city. Indeed, it is through the individual's movements and use of the city that the space is transformed into a place, i.e. a living space. With this, de Certeau illustrates the importance of theorising lived space, since it is through such spatial practices that social life is structured (2005, p. 96).

By shifting the focus of analysis from strategist to tactician and from city planner to city dweller, de Certeau directs our attention to how structures influence but can also be subverted by individual agency. The focus is thus on understanding how one is able to manoeuvre within these structures. It is through such creative manoeuvring that one can develop a certain, if limited, measure of autonomy in spite of the hegemonic structures of society (de

Space, Time, and the Urban Muslim 139

Certeau, 2005, p. 176). In the context of young Muslim's tours, de Certeau's perspective on space becomes an important avenue through which to understand these youths' attachments to their localities. The city is ingrained in their memories and pathways in the same way they, in turn, influence the city spaces through their presence and practices. In other words, it is through their everyday movements that young Muslims become an integral part of the city's heterogeneous spaces.

Temporalities of Spatial Biography: the Past, Present, and the (Potential) Future

The notion that our nostalgia is connected to a space set in a particular time is one of the most valuable insights of the tours I conducted with my Montreal participants. We remember and narrate our stories as they were set in and experienced in the past, regardless of how the physical space has changed since. However, as my participants took me to visit these sites of their key memories, they looked for what remained and what had changed. Noticing the changes, and reminiscing about how it used to be, highlights the nostalgia connected to a particular time and space that can only be reminisced about but never recreated. Yaqub's tour in Montreal demonstrates how spatial narratives can become important ways of constructing one's autobiography by moving through the spaces that represent past life experiences. Here, the spatial structures become avenues to the past. This was represented through Yaqub's spatial account. Going to his childhood home, visiting the mosque he used to attend, the malls, and restaurants; these spaces became a depiction of his lifelong connection to a particular locality within a Montreal suburb.

The narrative links Yaqub constructed as we moved from one place to another highlight how small-scale and localised movements can become part of a greater life storey, connecting spaces that are only linked through the personal meaning one attributes to them (Amit & Knowles, 2017). Such spatial narratives also demonstrate the construction of belonging to a locality. As Yaqub reminisced about playing hockey in his childhood home and the dents it created in the carport, he also called the present state of the space to become a witness of his past. As we moved through the spaces, they interchangeably either became witnesses to Yaqub's life narrative or displays of how these spaces exist irrespective of him. Public spaces can betray our personal connections as urban planners, social structures, or simply time and weather change the physical appearance of these spaces. As Yaqub demonstrated in his narrative, we are left with mere indicators of our memories and lost connections, yet we maintain their nostalgic significance through narrative.

Taking a different temporal approach to spatial narrative, Khadija in Copenhagen took me on a tour of her potential future. She took me to the Royal Theatre, the Opera House, up-scale restaurants. Most of these places she had only passed by on her walks through downtown Copenhagen. The

140   *Muslim Pathways and Spatial Narratives*

fact that Khadija did not have any social connection to these places at that moment of her tour was not the point. Rather, Khadija used the opportunity of her tour to construct an image of where she wanted to be in the future. The spatial narrative became an avenue to display her future self—a sort of futuristic spatial biography—tracing her future pathways through the city rather than her autobiographical pathways of her past. Khadija's spatial account demonstrated the potential for social representations of spaces to become significant in the construction of subjectivity. To Khadija, these spaces of Danish high culture and middle-class markers served to represent her aspirations for the future. The spaces represented Khadija's hope for her future social mobility, a social pathway she had already ventured on by starting a university degree that would ensure her a greater sense of financial comfort. With this futuristic spatial narrative, Khadija's tour displays the theoretical potential in investigating the temporal future through movements.

Historical accounts have long had a place in anthropological query. In an ethnographic sense, this has meant noting down life narratives as they were told by research participants and triangulating these accounts with archival data. Building on this ethnographic tradition, a broader understanding of mobility and the narratives that can be constructed through "moving" with people enables a different approach to temporal exploration. With this approach, the physical space becomes the triangulating proof of our interlocutors' narratives. It enables them to exercise greater epistemological influence to decide whether the focus of their life story should be placed in the past, present, or the future. Yaqub chose a spatial rendition of his past, in the form of his childhood and youthhood in suburban Montreal. Khadija depicted her potential future; this rendition of the future was open-ended. Her aspiration may be challenged in the future. She may struggle to find a well-paying job after finishing university or she may find other cultural interests than ballet and opera. Yet, with this future-orientated spatial account, Khadija not only displayed her future aspirations but also revealed her *expectation* of social mobility. This future was well within her reach, and depicting these spaces as potentially "hers," cemented her agency in making it happen.

Research on the future has often examined the notion of hope as the driving force for the future (Cole & Durham, 2008; Pedersen, 2012). However, it has often focused on marginalised actors who are in precarious situations, whether socially or financially, with limited potential to achieve the social mobility to which they aspire. This is not the case with Khadija. According to the racialised representation of Muslims in Denmark, Khadija, as a hijab-wearing young woman of immigrant background, represents a socioeconomically marginalised population group in Denmark. However, because of her social position as a university student and more importantly her own self-perception of belonging to a comfortable middle class, Khadija did not represent herself as marginalised and she did not see her social mobility as a vague distant hope. It was merely a matter of time and effort in establishing her career and financial security following graduation. In fact, her spatial

Space, Time, and the Urban Muslim 141

narrative seemed void of the typical uncertainty most young people would have about their futures (A. L. Dalsgaard & Frederiksen, 2013).

Both Yaqub and Khadija allowed me to discover the potential in spatial narratives as representations of temporality. The study of time has been a longstanding challenge for ethnographers (S. Dalsgaard & Nielsen, 2013). How do we observe and explore the meaning of time for social actors? When I designed this research project and included the method of touring the cities with young Muslims, I did not expect that I would be conducting an ethnography of time. Nevertheless—and to my surprise—my participants took my idea of urban tours and transformed it as a way to tell a story of time through a spatial narrative. Yaqub and Khadija demonstrate examples of how spatial stories can become a re-construction of one's past *and* a construction of one's potential future. It is easy to identify with Yaqub's visit to his childhood home and neighbourhood, observing its changes as well as what remains. Likewise, for any struggling young student, the dreams of Khadija—what she will do once she achieves financial stability—are all too familiar. While Yaqub's tour explored notions of memory and nostalgia, Khadija's tour explored notions of potential and hope. Their tours demonstrate how spatial narratives can be stories of what *was*, *is*, and (hopefully) *will be*. In these cases, the present is used as a temporal point of departure for either the past or the future.

Investigating Subjectivity through Spatial Accounts

Amy in Montreal and Dania in Copenhagen—although worlds apart in a geographical sense—share some significant similarities in their spatial accounts. Both came from small rural towns and moved to their new urban homes as they started university. In their tours, they exemplify the rural–urban migration many young people experience as they seek education and opportunities in the big cities. While similar in this regard, Amy and Dania also demonstrate the different approaches to rooting oneself in a new locality. How do you become an urbanite? What spaces do you seek to realise this process of becoming? Amy and Dania had different ways of constructing their belonging, and subsequently their movements. Yet both their tours exemplify the importance of subjectivity in the process of creating roots in a locality.

Amy took me on a walk through her local pathways, displaying her routinised walk through her neighbourhood. During our interview, she had shared with me the frustration of her rural upbringing and explained why she had come to view Montreal as her "home-city." Although a common perception of rural life is tranquillity and simplicity, for Amy, her life in a small rural town was too small, close-knit, and culturally uniform to allow her to fully explore who she could be. Throughout her tour, Amy seemed to have found more tranquillity in getting lost amidst the urban crowd of the busy high street close to her home than in her childhood town. The city's cultural and social diversity allowed Amy to discover herself and her artistic voice in a locality that not only allowed her alternative creative expressions

142   *Muslim Pathways and Spatial Narratives*

but commended her for it. It is through Amy's pathways that one comes to appreciate this urban becoming. She had constructed a sense of belonging to Montreal through these pathways. It was in this process that Amy also went through a process of *becoming* a Montrealer. This process of becoming an urbanite was narrated through her emotional and creative attachments to the city spaces on her tour. Following her graduation from university, she went on to pursue postgraduate studies in the United Kingdom, after which she moved on to a university position in a different country. Her initial migration from rural Ontario to Montreal was only the first stop on the larger transnational migration pathways that ensued. However, in many ways, it was this initial rural–urban migration and the localised movements that constructed her urban subjectivity. In turn, this made the global cities she moved to so attractive to her. Amy's transnational mobility demonstrates how movements are often a series of moves "from the countryside to the city, within geopolitical regions, across state and regional borders, visits back and forth across dispersed social networks, return migration" (Amit & Olwig, 2011, p. 4). The focus is here on the wide range of moves people may make throughout their lives. As Amy's improvised movements depict, there is an increasing awareness of how "moving people construct and *re*construct places, social relations and social contexts in the course of and through their ongoing experiences of movement" (Amit & Olwig, 2011, p. 4). Now, years after our walk in Montreal, I can see how Amy's ability to navigate opportunities as they presented themselves to her enabled her current internationally mobile lifestyle. Her narrative demonstrates how people's movements must be contextualised within a broader understanding of their lives, their aspirations, as well as their social ties and socioeconomic privileges.

Dania focused her tour on taking me to her favourite neighbourhood, not necessarily where she lived (in the more affluent Frederiksberg) but where she "expresses herself" in the trendy part of Nørrebro. It is in this expression of how she wanted to be perceived that the process of urban becoming is displayed. Like Amy, it was through her choice of spaces in her tour that Dania constructed a particular version of her subjectivity. This subjectivity emphasised her seamless integration into the urban landscape. While her hijab and ethnicity would stick out as out of the ordinary in her rural Danish town, in Nørrebro, her appearance became incorporated into broader public representations of Nørrebro's cultural diversity and inclusivity. Thus, she was not only affected by the process of becoming urban, but her very subjectivity became incorporated into the social landscape that defines Nørrebro's public image.

Like Amy, Dania was preparing to go abroad for a semester as part of her university degree. As she described her trip, she was excited at the prospects, yet she was sure that it would only be a temporary experience. The ultimate goal was to settle in Copenhagen. The major and life-changing migration for her would be her rural-urban migration; the process of becoming a Copenhagener was more representative of how she saw herself. Her travels

Space, Time, and the Urban Muslim   143

and exploring the world outside of Copenhagen and Denmark were temporary mobilities, and never intended as places to settle in.

Amy and Dania's spatial narratives are in fact migration narratives. Rural–urban migration is one of the longest standing examples of human migration, and these two examples demonstrate the process of adapting to and adopting one's new urban locality. They both had sought the cultural and social diversity of big cities, and they both displayed an image of themselves as urbanites, understating their rural backgrounds. Indeed, it is interesting to note in Amy and Dania's spatial accounts how little importance they accorded their rural backgrounds. For instance, they both took me to their favourite park, where they went to escape the urban chaos. However, this was not explained as a longing for their rural homes (although that may have been the case). Rather, they both explained it as a break from the hustle and bustle of the city. This is noteworthy because it is through their constructed relation to the city, rather than through a nostalgic connection to their rural homes, that they emphasised their urban belonging.

Amy and Dania's cases depict the subject-constructing process of rural–urban migration that many young people experience. Through their years in Montreal and Copenhagen, respectively, they have chosen certain pathways, neighbourhoods, and streets as part of their habitual being-in-the-city that allowed them to construct certain versions of themselves as young, well-educated, culturally explorative, and socially conscious urbanites. It is in these choices, and ultimately in the choice of representing themselves through their spatial narratives as inhabitants rooted in these two cities, that they construct their urban subjectivities. Nevertheless, Amy and Dania's spatial narratives are only one example of how subjectivities are displayed through routinised pathways. In fact, whether my participants focused their spatial accounts on their life stories, future aspirations, or present social positions, these accounts were always an expression of their agency in constructing and representing certain subjectivities.

Mobility and Movements as Meaning-Making Processes

So far in this chapter, I have drawn analytical comparisons between some of the young Muslims I met in Montreal and Copenhagen. These comparisons allow us to appreciate the differences and similarities that spatial narratives highlight. As previously mentioned, I relinquished a degree of my ethnographic power when I asked my interlocutors to take me on a tour of their city. I left the question broad and open to their interpretation. This resulted in rich ethnographic material depicting my interlocutors' unique histories, social positions, and subjectivities. Participating in their movements while listening to their reasoning and narratives for imbuing certain spaces with particular importance—and sometimes undermining other spaces' importance—put my interlocutors in a broader structural context, where they were able to display their agency through their narrative choices. They chose

144 *Muslim Pathways and Spatial Narratives*

the spaces we walked through, the direction we went, and which stories of the past, imaginaries of the future, or their social image in the present they wanted to highlight.

The interviews I had conducted with all of them before their spatial tours only demonstrated one side of their lives. The interviews were limited by my own analytical scope, what I thought was important to ask about, and what I thought was important to represent. As with all ethnographers, the question of ethnographic representation, doing justice to the complex lives and subjectivities of our interlocutors, always lingers. The tours I conducted incorporated young Muslims in the epistemological process of ethnography. They were doing ethnography with me, and they were instilling this ethnography with analytical potential through their narratives and reflections as we were walking through their city spaces.

Let me return to my friend, Lisa, whom I introduced at the beginning of this chapter. She felt she had taken part in my research not just as a participant, but as a collaborator. Therefore, it was satisfying for both her and me to be able to share analytical ideas about the tour on which she had taken me. Lisa allowed me to incorporate her into the early stages of processing my ethnographic material following the conclusion of my fieldwork. By inviting her to share her thoughts on my research, she put my research in a wider literary framework comparing it to the cultural significance of aboriginal walkabouts. Like the aboriginal walkabout, the walk she took me on had a cultural, social, and personal significance to her.

Moving away from the limiting perspectives of traditional mobility research as a linear movement from point A to point B allows for the complexities of different types of movements to be appreciated. In their tours, Lisa and my other participants in Montreal and Copenhagen demonstrated the complexities of movements through seemingly random pathways and places. However, their aimlessness was instilled with meaning through their narratives as we walked while they explained the significance of particular spaces. Returning to Henrik Vigh's (2009) definition of social navigation that I introduced in the "Introduction" helps us appreciate the complex navigation skills of young Muslims in these two cities. While Vigh's work focuses on youth in Guinea Bissau that have little chance of achieving social mobility because of limiting social structures, the young Muslims I met were privileged because of their social capital in navigating their social terrains. My participants navigated the streets of their city, informing me of our next destination on their tour, explaining its place in their life story. With this, they depicted their agency not only in navigating the physical structures and spaces of their city, but just as much in the social terrain that provided opportunities or challenges as they moved through their daily lives.

These tours were a moving representation of young Muslims' subjectivity realised through their individual choices. With these choices, they made certain spaces and pathways part of their daily routines, while simultaneously representing a certain version of their rootedness, social mobility,

Space, Time, and the Urban Muslim 145

and prospects as localised in these city spaces and paths. Amit and Knowles (2017) argue that such navigation strategies display life stories in mobile-spatial terms—what they call spatial biography. Some of my participants did exactly that. They took me on a journey of their past as witnessed by the spaces through which they created these memories. Lisa, for instance, took me on a walk of Old Pointe Claire Village in the West Island of Montreal. This walk was a recurring destination throughout her childhood and teenage years. When her grandmother visited from Scotland as a child, they would share an ice cream as they walked through the village and nearby lake. When she got a job as a teenager at a nearby community organic store, she would take that walk on her own. Later in life, it was a place in which to celebrate national holidays and see the fireworks with family or friends. The pathways she took me on displayed the various meanings the spaces had at different times in her life. They were not simply a temporal account of her connection to the spaces. The spaces were, however, instilled with different meanings at different times in her life. It was through the spatial narrative that she constructed these various meanings:

> My love for this place started when I was a kid and my grandmother would visit from Scotland, and she loves to take walks and to look into the stores, "have a rake", she would call it. So kinda like sorting through stuff seeing what's there. Not necessarily buying anything, just looking. So, we would take the bus together, come here, walk, get ice

Figure 6.1 The Saint Lawrence River at Old Pointe Claire Village, West Island, Montreal.

146 *Muslim Pathways and Spatial Narratives*

cream, go down to the water, and sit. My grandmother came pretty regularly up until I was 10–11. She would come at least once a year and sometimes more [but then] my grandfather's knees got bad [they got too old to travel].

Later in my teens, I would like to come and go down to the water. Sometimes if I had to, like, think of something, or there was a couple of times I had stuff that troubled me, I would like to come to the water and just sit and think. So even before I was Muslim and since I became Muslim, it's just a favourite spot to go if I just need to clear my mind and work things out. It's my little spot. And then also, they have Canada Day celebration here and St Jean Baptiste. So they have a festival here and big fireworks, it's very nice.

I feel like it's mostly the same [as my childhood], but what it means for me has changed slightly over time. So, before it was a place where my grandmother used to take me. After that it was the cooperative café that sold the organic stuff where I could find a community, people who were likeminded and I could share ideas with. It became a place for me where I could come and think and see unique stores, it wasn't like big corporations. I think, they have some kind of board where they don't allow franchises to this area, or else for sure it would be. So, they do protect the area from corporations.

(Lisa, Montreal)

I highlight this segment of Lisa's walk here because it displays the meaning-making process of spatial biographies. How the past is reinterpreted through the present, highlighting the multiple interpretations and meanings, instilled in certain spaces and pathways through a temporal analytical gaze. Lisa had thought about where she wanted to take me, what spaces of her past she wanted to emphasise, and what memories from her past were important to highlight as a continuous meaningful life narrative. For Lisa, who is a Muslim convert, this continuity in her life course was important to emphasise through her tour. Her choice to become Muslim was an extension of the person she was and is becoming, and she wanted to emphasise this through her spatial biography, creating links between her past and her present. The fact that Old Pointe Claire had changed in meaning throughout her life did not minimise its importance. Rather, it was a point of continuity in her life narrative, its meaning evolving with her through time. This is especially possible because Old Pointe Claire village had not changed significantly since her childhood. So, it became a symbol of continuity in Lisa's life that had involved major life changes.

Conclusion

The ethnographic exploration of movement and spatial narrative can have multiple functions. First, through spatial accounts that emphasise subjective

Space, Time, and the Urban Muslim   147

choices and self-reflexivity, my participants constructed their own stories and self-representations. They ultimately demonstrated their ability to navigate city spaces, both physically and socially. These spatial narratives provided young Muslims with the potential to represent themselves, their connection to their city, and their own self-image through movements. Second, these movements provided ethnographic insight into my participants' unique experiences, complex lives, and personal identifications. They were all young, between the ages of 18 and 25, from Montreal or Copenhagen, and self-identified as Muslims. However, their spatial narratives beyond these similar shared identifications demonstrate the extensive and important nuances that pose implicit questions about the nature of ethnographic representation.

How can we, as ethnographers, explore the lives of people who share certain categorical identifications (in this case: being Muslim, young, and urban) without an *a priori* assumption of groupness, and thus risk reducing the lived complexity to simplistic representation (Brubaker, 2004). Following my participants' local pathways—considering the temporal and the social aspects of their narratives—highlights how a focus on spatial narratives provided young Muslims with a narrative tool that allowed them to demonstrate more nuances than they could depict in the qualitative interviews or even through my participation in their social and political events. Although these other ethnographic tools did provide insights into their histories and everyday priorities, it was the spatial accounts that allowed for their own agency and subjectivity to be expressed.

Conclusion
Navigating Colour-Blind Societies

It has been almost a decade since I started my fieldwork in Denmark and Canada. The young people I met in Copenhagen and Montreal have since graduated, started families, migrated to other countries or cities, and continued on with their lives. When I met these youth in their early 20s, their everyday lives and movements through the city were influenced by their social position, their young adulthood, as well as their self-ascribed identification as Muslim Copenhageners/Montrealers. They had plans and hopes for their future; imaginings of how they would configure the city spaces to match these hopes and aspirations. But life often presents different opportunities and expectations that can drastically change pathways in different directions as well as different political and social consciousnesses. These natural evolutions in their life course demonstrate the value of conducting longitudinal studies with emerging adults.

By choosing to research young people who self-identify as Muslim, I have run the risk of reproducing the overemphasis of "Muslim" as an important signifier that differentiates my interlocutors from their social contexts. However, I use my interlocutors' self-ascribed Muslim label to explore the ways they themselves reproduce this identification and negotiate different ways of incorporating it into societies in which their Muslimness may often be viewed as a foreign element, but for themselves is an engrained part of their urban localised lives. This book is thus an attempt to discuss how ethnographers can represent people who are reified by populist rhetoric and sometimes even by themselves without reproducing such reification in our research. In many ways, I take an optimistic approach towards the lives of the young Muslims I met in Copenhagen and Montreal. I argue for their ability to circumvent racialising assemblages by navigating and using social spaces to enforce a representation of belonging. My participants creatively incorporated hegemonic cultural elements (style, speech, representations) that would ease their upward social mobility, while simultaneously resisting in various ways Islamophobic rhetoric that sought to marginalise them. Such agency to contest their otherisation was only possible because of their own representations of belonging. They embodied these representations in their interviews and spatial tours, which in turn localised them within their cities.

DOI: 10.4324/9781003294696-10

Conclusion 149

Comparative Ethnography

Through a comparative transatlantic perspective, this book expands our understanding of the complex lives of young Muslims in colour-blind societies. The book includes perspectives on how racialisation processes exist in contexts that erase the significance of race while still upholding racial hierarchies. By including a critical sociopolitical and urban analysis to a phenomenological approach of understanding Muslims' experiences, I examine the various repercussions of framing the Muslim as the quintessential Other in Denmark and Quebec.

Copenhagen and Montreal are diverse cities, yet they exist in national/provincial contexts where cultural, religious, ethnic differences are erased. I challenge the racialisation of Muslims within these societies and the emphasis on their foreignness *qua* their Muslimness. The reification of Muslims through racialisation processes overlooks the fluid, processual, and situational characteristics of young Muslims' identification. Besides being Muslim, my participants identified as urban, young, and middle class—all important in their everyday lives.

The book interrogates the complex circumstances through which young Muslims may feel limited by Islamophobic political rhetoric that ripples into everyday interactions. Nevertheless, they find alternative ways of navigating through such racialised assemblages. Throughout this book, I explore young Muslims' creative efforts to navigate through the assumption of their otherness through self-representation and the use of spatial narratives. While young Muslims in these two cities may actively resist Islamophobic policies and social exclusion, they also creatively express their localised Danish or Canadian Muslimness.

Navigating colour-blind societies

Both Denmark and Quebec are imagined to be post-racial societies in political and popular imagination. They are beyond "race"—they are colour-blind. I use the idea of colour-blindness here to present a critical analysis of how racialisation processes occur in such societies. How do you navigate a society that others you, yet refuses to acknowledge the racist underpinnings of this otherisation? In such a society, the racialisation of Muslims as foreigners and even a potential threat to societal values becomes normative. It creates ripples throughout society, from powerful political discourse to mundane everyday encounters.

To understand the process of racialisation in colour-blind societies, I employ the idea of assemblages. This concept is helpful as it leads us away from pre-emptive assumptions of power dynamics and resistance, towards an understanding of how different societal entities are interconnected. Looking at assemblages of racialisation thus opens for an exploration of racialisation processes as they are formulated in political, social, and spatial fields.

150   *Conclusion*

Furthermore, it allows us to interrogate how these processes affect young Muslims differently based on their intersecting identifications such as class, religiosity, gender, etc. In other words, Muslim racialisation encompasses many different potentials.

The first part of the book focuses on social navigation as a tactic to circumvent and contest racialisation processes in social interactions. The second part of the book looks closer at how young Muslims navigate through urban spaces to construct spatial narratives. These spatial narratives were ways of constructing and representing their belonging to their cities and rooting them within their city spaces. Furthermore, the narratives became implicit ways of contesting cartographies of racialisation and political otherisation. No one can argue with the spatial biographies through which young Montreal Muslims narrate themselves into the history of their cities. Similarly, for Danish Muslims, the ease with which they navigated through city spaces enabled them challenge spatial racialisation and cement their class position as middle-class Danish Muslims. They thus exhibit the interrelation between racialisation and spatialisation processes. Throughout this book, the main argument has been to demonstrate how both social and physical spaces provide complex terrains and opportunities for navigating racialisation assemblages.

Throughout the book, I complexify the idea of agency and resistance. Building on Mahmood's work, I situate the concept of agency within the limits of particular political and social contexts. Agency is thus a capacity to act with limited possibilities to resist hegemonic structures. In the Danish context, the middle-class Muslims I met navigated society's racial formations, their social mobility, and middle-class positioning. Their use of middle-class respectability markers should not be understood as being apologetic of their Muslimness. Rather, within the limited space of resistance afforded to them, these youth understood how to utilise their social capital to resist the process of racialisation. Through academic, professional, and socioeconomic successes, they knew how to challenge racist assumptions of their inferiority and otherness expressed in everyday encounters.

The reification of visible signifiers of Muslimness in many Western paradigms, often targeting women, is an important part of the racialisation of Muslims as a quintessential Other. In the Quebec context, this has led to the prohibition of hijab and niqab. Emphasising the Muslim experience of the hijab debate, I demonstrated how Muslims' self-representation is a way of constructing the group, but also risks reproducing a Western reification of Muslimness (i.e. by giving supremacy to the hijab as a signifier of Islam). By approaching social groups as something to analyse, I build on the work of Rogers Brubaker. Muslim groupness then is a social phenomenon to be analysed, one that is continuously recreated and maintained through social and religious events as well as public representations. By approaching social groups as objects of analysis rather than analytical objects, we can expose the

Conclusion 151

nuances, complexities, and diversity among people who claim a shared sense of community.

Complicating Muslim Belonging

The comparative ethnographic approach of this book emphasises both the similarities and differences between Muslims in Copenhagen and Montreal. Comparative research is challenging with time and travel constraints, but its benefits are undeniable; it allows the researcher to gain a broader perspective on local issues.

By exploring the racialising and socially complex realities experienced by young Muslims in their urban localities, I go beyond the socially and politically constructed dichotomy of "Muslim Them" versus "Western Us." Throughout this book, I do not represent young Muslims as part of a distinct community separate from their broader societies but as young Copenhageners and Montrealers who self-identify as Muslims, and who must improvise alternative ways of navigating being Muslim, young, and urban at the same time.

Working from a theoretical framework inspired by Michel de Certeau and Henri Lefebvre, this book contributes to our understanding of how urban spaces play into our lives. It provides an important contribution to our understanding of young Muslims' urban lives in appreciating the complex reality that shapes young people's agency and social relations. By exploring the urban pathways of my participants, I contribute to the theoretical discussions within mobility and urban studies. The ways young Muslims represent themselves through spatial narratives contributes to our understanding of social spaces, considering both the temporal and social representation of particular streets and districts, and using these to emphasise one's position. My participants demonstrated their rootedness within their cities through the spatial narratives they constructed. It is through such spatial representations that they inadvertently depicted their belonging in stark opposition to racialising political discourse that seeks to represent them as "Others."

References

Abu-Lughod, L. (1990). The romance of resistance: Tracing transformations of power through Bedouin women. *American Ethnologist, 17*(1), 41–55.

Abu-Lughod, L. (2013). *Do Muslim women need saving?* Harvard University Press.

Ahmed, S. (2000). *Strange encounters: Embodied others in post-coloniality.* Psychology Press.

Al-Shamasnah, F., & Hammoude, J. (2023). Mand, Muslim og Minoritet: Oplevede Positioneringer og Håndteringsstrategier blandt Etniske Minoritetsmænd med Muslimsk Baggrund [Man, Muslim and Minority: Experienced Positionalities and Coping Strategies among Minority Ethnic Men with Muslim Background]. *Scandinavian Journal of Islamic Studies, 17*(1), Article 1. https://doi.org/10.7146/tifo.v17i1.137280

Amit, V. (2002). *Realizing community: Concepts, social relationships and sentiments.* Psychology Press.

Amit, V. (2010). Community as 'good to think with': The productiveness of strategic ambiguities. *Anthropologica, 52*(2), 357–363.

Amit, V., & Knowles, C. (2017). Improvising and navigating mobilities: Tacking in everyday life. *Theory, Culture & Society, 34*(7–8), 165–179.

Amit, V., & Olwig, K. F. (2011). Introduction to 'changes of place: Interrogating the continuities and disjunctures of movement'. *Anthropologica, 53*(1), 3–7.

Amit-Talai, V. (1994). Urban pathways: The logistics of youth peer relations. In Vered Amit-Talai and Henri Lustiger-Thaler (Eds.) *Urban lives: Fragmentation and resistance* (pp. 183–205). McClelland & Stewart.

Anctil, P. (2011). Reasonable accommodation in the Canadian legal context: A mechanism for handling diversity or a source of tension? In H. Adelman & P. Anctil (Eds.), *Religion, culture, and the state: Reflections on the Bouchard-Taylor report* (pp. 16–36). University of Toronto Press.

Andersen, T. K., & Reiermann, J. (2019). Hver fjerde dansker: Muslimer skal ud af Danmark [Every Fourth Dane: Muslims Must Leave Denmark]. *Mandag Morgen.* https://www.mm.dk/artikel/hver-fjerde-dansker-muslimer-skal-ud-af-danmark (Accessed: 13/10/2023).

Anderson, B. (2006). *Imagined communities: Reflections on the origin and spread of nationalism.* Verso Books.

Anderson, E. (2022). *Black in White space.* University of Chicago Press.

Andreassen, R., & Vitus, K. (2016). Introduction: Affectivity as a lens to racial formations in the Nordic countries. In R. Andreassen and K. Vitus (Eds.) *Affectivity and race* (pp. 11–28). Routledge.

154 *References*

Austin, D. (2010). Narratives of power: Historical mythologies in contemporary Quebec and Canada. *Race & Class*, 52(1), 19–32.

Bakali, N. (2015). Contextualising the Quebec charter of values: How the Muslim 'Other' is conceptualised in Quebec. *Culture and Religion*, 16(4), 412–429.

Benhadjoudja, L. (2017). Laïcité narrative et sécularonationalisme au Québec à l'épreuve de la race, du genre et de la sexualité [Secularism Narratives and Secular Nationalism in Quebec challenged by race, gender and sexuality]. *Studies in Religion/Sciences Religieuses*, 46(2), 272–291.

Bhattacharyya, G. (2009). *Dangerous brown men: Exploiting sex, violence and feminism in the 'war on terror'*. Bloomsbury Publishing.

Bilge, S. (2013). Reading the racial subtext of the Québécois accommodation controversy: An analytics of racialized governmentality. *Politikon*, 40(1), 157–181.

Bonilla-Silva, E. (1997). Rethinking racism: Toward a structural interpretation. *American Sociological Review*, 63(2), 465–480.

Bonilla-Silva, E. (2001). *White supremacy and racism in the post-civil rights era*. Lynne Rienner Publishers.

Bonilla-Silva, E. (2006). *Racism without racists: Color-blind racism and the persistence of racial inequality in the United States*. Rowman & Littlefield Publishers.

Bouchard, G., & Taylor, C. (2008). *Building The Future: A time for reconciliation, abridged report*. Bibliothèque et Archives nationales du Québec.

Brubaker, R. (2002). Ethnicity without groups. *European Journal of Sociology/ Archives Européennes de Sociologie*, 43(2), 163–189.

Brubaker, R. (2004). *Ethnicity without groups*. Harvard University Press.

Christensen, C. D., & Stræde, J. C. (2016). *Indvandrere og efterkommere stryger til tops på arbejdsmarkedet [Immigrants and Descendants Rise to the Top in the Labour Market]*. Mandag Morgen. https://www.mm.dk/artikel/indvandrere-og -efterkommere-stryger-til-tops-paa-arbejdsmarkedet (Accessed: 13/10/2023).

Cole, J., & Durham, D. L. (2008). Introduction: Globalization and the temporality of children and youth. In J. Cole & D. L. Durham (Eds.), *Figuring the future: Globalization and the temporalities of children and youth* (pp. 3–24). School for Advanced Research Press.

Cooper, A. (2007). *The hanging of Angélique: The untold story of Canadian slavery and the burning of old Montreal*. University of Georgia Press.

Crenshaw, K. (1990). Mapping the margins: Intersectionality, identity politics, and violence against women of color. *Stanford Law Review*, 43, 1241.

Crenshaw, K. (2018). *Demarginalizing the intersection of race and sex: A Black feminist critique of antidiscrimination doctrine, feminist theory, and antiracist politics [1989]*. Routledge.

Dahl, K. M., & Jakobsen, V. (2005). *Køn, etnicitet og barrierer for integration [Gender, Ethnicity and Barriers for Integration]*. The Danish National Centre for Social Research.

Dalsgaard, A. L., & Frederiksen, M. D. (2013). Out of conclusion: On recurrence and open-endedness in life and analysis. *Social Analysis*, 57(1), 50.

Dalsgaard, S., & Nielsen, M. (2013). Introduction: Time and the field. *Social Analysis*, 57(1),1-19.

Dastageer, K. (2013). Nydansker? Jeg er da ikke ny i Danmark! [New Dane? I'm Not New in Denmark] .*Politiken*. https://politiken.dk/debat/debatindlaeg/art5512535/ Nydansker-Jeg-er-da-ikke-ny-i-Danmark (Accessed: 13/10/2023).

References 155

Dazey, M. (2021). Rethinking respectability politics. *The British Journal of Sociology*, 72(3), 580–593.

De Certeau, M. (2005). The practice of everyday life. In G. M. Spiegel, (Ed.) *Practicing history: New directions in historical writing after the linguistic turn* (pp. 217–228). Routledge.

Du Bois, W. E. B. (2008). *The souls of Black folk*. Oxford University Press.

El-Tayeb, F. (2011). *European others: Queering ethnicity in postnational Europe*. University of Minnesota Press.

Fadil, N. (2010). Breaking the taboo of multiculturalism. The Belgian left and Islam. In S. Sayyid & A. Vakil (Eds.), *Thinking through Islamophobia: Global perspectives*. Hurst & Columbia University Press.

Finnegan, R. (1989). *The hidden musicians: Music making in an English town*. Cambridge University Press.

Fossum, J. E. (2009). *The ties that bind: Accommodating diversity in Canada and the European Union*. Peter Lang.

Folketinget.(2017).*V 38 Om antal beboere i Brøndby Strand med indvandrerbaggrund* [V 38 About the number of residents in Brøndby Strand with immigrant background.] Parliament Hearing. https://www.ft.dk/samling/20161/vedtagelse/v38/index.htm.

Frederiksen, M. (2014, April 2). *Fællesskabet er det særlige ved Danmark [Community is what is special about Denmark]*. Berlingske.dk. https://www.berlingske.dk/content/item/246546 (Accessed: 13/10/2023).

Frederiksen, M. (2020). *Statsminister Mette Frederiksens tale ved Folketingets åbning den 6. Oktober 2020 [Prime Minister Mette Frederiksen's speech at the Opening of the Parliament on 6th October 2020]*. Statsministeriet. https://www.stm.dk/statsministeren/taler/statsminister-mette-frederiksens-tale-ved-folketingets-aabning-den-6-oktober-2020/ (Accessed: 13/10/2023).

Freiesleben, A. M. (2016). *Et Danmark af parallelsamfund [One Denmark without Parallel Societies]*. PhD ThesisUniversity of Copenhagen.

Freiwald, B. T. (2011). 'Qui est nous?' Some answers from the Bouchard-Taylor Commision's archive. In H. Adelman & P. Anctil (Eds.), *Religion, culture, and the state: Reflections on the Bouchard-Taylor report* (pp. 69–85). University of Toronto Press.

Garner, S., & Selod, S. (2015). The racialization of Muslims: Empirical studies of Islamophobia. *Critical Sociology*, 41(1), 9–19.

Ghumkhor, S. (2019). *The political psychology of the veil: The impossible body*. Springer.

Gilroy, P. (2004). *After empire* (Vol. 105). Routledge.

Gilroy, P. (2013). *There ain't no Black in the Union Jack*. Routledge.

Goldberg, D. T. (2006). Racial Europeanization. *Ethnic and Racial Studies*, 29(2), 331–364.

Goul, J. A. (2002). Danskernes holdninger til indvandrere. En oversigt [Danes' attitudes towards immigrants. An overview]. *AMID, Institut for Historie, Internationale Studier Og Samfundsforhold*, 1–31.

Grillo, R. D. (2003). Cultural essentialism and cultural anxiety. *Anthropological Theory*, 3(2), 157–173.

Gullestad, M. (2002). Invisible fences: Egalitarianism, nationalism and racism. *Journal of the Royal Anthropological Institute*, 8(1), 45–63.

156   References

Habib, S. (2017). *Learning and teaching British values: Policies and perspectives on British identities*. Springer.

Hafiz, M. (2022). *Can Muslims think?: Race, Islam, and the end of Europe*. Rowman & Littlefield.

Hallam, E., & Ingold, T. (2021). *Creativity and cultural improvisation*. Routledge.

Hannerz, U., & Ulf Hannerz, H. (1996). *Transnational connections: Culture, people, places*. Taylor & Francis US.

Hassani, A. (2023a). Racialisation in a "raceless" nation: Muslims navigating Islamophobia in Denmark's everyday life. In A. Groglopo and J. Suárez-Krabbe (Eds.) *Coloniality and decolonisation in the Nordic region* (pp. 37–50). Routledge.

Hassani, A. (2023b). Convivial narratives as agency: Middle-class Muslims evading racialisation in Copenhagen. *The Sociological Review*. Advance online publication. https://doi.org/10.1177/00380261231184356

Henkel, H. (2010). Fundamentally Danish? The Muhammad cartoon crisis as transitional drama. *Human Architecture*, 8(2), 67.

Hervik, P. (2004). The Danish cultural world of unbridgeable differences. *Ethnos*, 69(2), 247–267.

Hervik, P. (2019). Racialization in the Nordic countries: An introduction. In *Racialization, racism, and anti-racism in the Nordic countries* (pp. 3–37). Springer.

Higginbotham, E. B. (1993). *Righteous discontent: The women's movement in the Black Baptist church, 1880–1920*. American Mathematical Soc.

The Danish Institute for Human Rights. (2022, March 19). *Etnisk profilering* [Ethnic Profiling]. The Danish Institute for Human Rights. https://menneskeret.dk/udgivelser/etnisk-profilering

Jackson, M. (1996). *Things as they are: New directions in phenomenological anthropology*. Georgetown University Press.

Jacques Parizeau, Quebec referendum, 1995. (2020, October 29). *Great Canadian speeches*. https://greatcanadianspeeches.ca/2020/10/29/jacques-parizeau-quebec -referendum-1995/

Jenkins, R. (2011). *Being Danish: Paradoxes of identity in everyday life*. Museum Tusculanum Press.

Jensen, L. (2018). *Postcolonial Denmark: Nation narration in a crisis ridden Europe*. Routledge.

Khawaja, I. (2011). Blikkene: Muslimskhedens synlighed, kropsliggørelse og forhandling [The Gazes: The Visibility, Embodiment and Negotiation of Muslimness]. In M.H. Pedersen and M. Rytter (Eds.), *Islam og muslimer i Danmark. Religion, identitet og sikkerhed efter 11. september 2001 [Islam and Muslims in Denmark. Religion, Identity and Security after 11th September 2001]* (pp. 269–292). Museum Tussulanmus Forlag.

Knowles, C. (2000). *Bedlam on the streets*. Routledge.

Knowles, C. (2003). *Race and social analysis*. Sage.

Knowles, C. (2010). Mobile sociology. *The British Journal of Sociology*, 61(s1), 373–379.

Knowles, C. (2011). Cities on the move: Navigating urban life. *City*, 15(2), 135–153.

Koefoed, L. (2015). Majority and minority nationalism in the Danish post-welfare state. *Geografiska Annaler: Series B, Human Geography*, 97(3), 223–232.

Kublitz, A. (2010). The cartoon controversy: Creating Muslims in a Danish setting. *Social Analysis*, 54(3), 107.

References   157

Larsen, A. (2000). Etnisk diskrimination, ligestilling og integration på arbejdsmarkedet [Ethnic discrimination, equality and integration in the labor market]. *Tidsskrift for Arbejdsliv*, 2(2), 67–83.

Lefebvre, H. (2014). *The production of space (1991)*. Routledge.

Lentin, A. (2008). Europe and the silence about race. *European Journal of Social Theory*, 11(4), 487–503.

Liep, J. (2001). *Locating cultural creativity*. Pluto Press.

Mahmood, S. (2011). *Politics of piety: The Islamic revival and the feminist subject*. Princeton University Press.

Mahrouse, G. (2010). 'Reasonable accommodation' in Québec: The limits of participation and dialogue. *Race & Class*, 52(1), 85–96.

Mahrouse, G. (2018). Minimizing and denying racial violence: Insights from the Québec mosque shooting. *Canadian Journal of Women and the Law*, 30(3), 471–493. https://doi.org/10.3138/cjwl.30.3.006

Maillé, C., & Salée, D. (2013). Quebec, secularism and women's rights: On feminism and Bill 94. In C. Maillé, G. Nielsen, & D. Salée (Eds.), *Revealing democracy: Secularism and religion in liberal democratic states* (pp. 11–34). PIE Peter Lang.

Mamdani, M. (2005). *Good Muslim, bad Muslim: America, the Cold War, and the roots of terror*. Harmony.

Massey, D. (2013). *Space, place and gender*. John Wiley & Sons.

Massoumi, N., Mills, T., & Miller, D. (Eds.). (2017). *What is Islamophobia?: Racism, social movements and the state*. Pluto Press.

Mikkelsen, B. (2005). *Tale ved Det Konservative Folkepartis landsmøde [Speech at the Conservative People's Party national meeting]*. https://www.dansketaler.dk/tale/landsmoedet-2005/ (Accessed: 13/10/2023).

Mondon, A., & Winter, A. (2020). *Reactionary democracy: How racism and the populist far right became mainstream*. Verso Books.

Neely, B., & Samura, M. (2011). Social geographies of race: Connecting race and space. *Ethnic and Racial Studies*, 34(11), 1933–1952.

Norton, A. (2013). *On the Muslim question*. Princeton University Press.

Odumosu, T. (2019). What lies unspoken: A remedy for colonial silence (s) in Denmark. *Third Text*, 33(4–5), 615–629.

Olsen, T. L. (2018). Inger Støjberg efter V-kritik af håndtryk: 'Ingen er tvunget til at blive dansker' [Inger Støjberg after V criticism of handshakes: 'No one is forced to become a Dane']. *DR*. https://www.dr.dk/nyheder/politik/inger-stoejberg-efter-v-kritik-af-haandtryk-ingen-er-tvunget-til-blive-dansker (Accessed: 13/10/2023).

Olwig, K. F. (2003). Narrating deglobalization: Danish perceptions of a lost empire. *Global Networks*, 3(3), 207–222.

Olwig, K. F., & Pærregaard, K. (2011). Introduction: "Strangers" in the nation. In K. F. Olwig (Ed.), *The question of integration: Immigration, exclusion and the Danish welfare state* (pp. 1–28). Cambridge Scholars Publishing, in press Newcastle.

Omi, M., & Winant, H. (2014). *Racial formation in the United States*. Routledge.

Open Society Justice Initiative. (2022). *How the EU is failing Muslim women*. https://www.justiceinitiative.org/publications/restrictions-on-muslim-women-s-dress-in-the-27-eu-member-states-and-the-united-kingdom

Overgaard, S. (2020). Facing eviction, residents of Denmark's 'Ghettos' are suing the government. *NPR.Org*. https://www.npr.org/2020/08/15/900874510/facing-eviction-residents-of-denmarks-ghettos-are-suing-the-government (Accessed: 13/10/2023).

158 References

Pedersen, M. A. (2012). A day in the Cadillac: The work of hope in urban Mongolia. *Social Analysis*, 56(2), 136–151.

Puar, J. (2013). Rethinking homonationalism. *International Journal of Middle East Studies*, 45(2), 336–339.

Puar, J. K. (2018). *Terrorist assemblages: Homonationalism in queer times*. Duke University Press.

Puar, J. K. (2020). "I Would Rather be a Cyborg than a Goddess": Becoming-intersectional in assemblage theory. In C. McCann, K. Seung-kyung, Emek Ergun (Eds.) *Feminist theory reader* (5th ed.). Routledge.

Puwar, N. (2004). *Space invaders: Race, gender and bodies out of place*. Berg.

Razack, S. (2002). *Race, space, and the law: Unmapping a White settler society*. Between the Lines.

Razack, S. H. (2004). Imperilled Muslim women, dangerous Muslim men and civilised Europeans: Legal and social responses to forced marriages. *Feminist Legal Studies*, 12(2), 129–174. https://doi.org/10.1023/B:FEST.0000043305.66172.92

Regeringen. (2018). *Ét Danmark uden parallelsamfund—Ingen ghettoer i 2030 [One Denmark without parallel societies—No ghettos in 2030]* . Government report.

Rostbøll, C. F. (2010). Indvandring, offentlig mening og politisk teori [Immigration, public opinion and political theory]. *Politik*, 13(2),26-35. https://doi.org/10.7146/politik.v13i2.27447

Rytter, M. (2010). 'The Family of Denmark' and 'the Aliens': Kinship images in Danish integration politics. *Ethnos*, 75(3), 301–322. https://doi.org/10.1080/00141844.2010.513773

Rytter, M. (2019). Writing against integration: Danish imaginaries of culture, race and belonging. *Ethnos*, 84(4), 678–697. https://doi.org/10.1080/00141844.2018.1458745

Rytter, M., & Pedersen, M. H. (2014). A decade of suspicion: Islam and Muslims in Denmark after 9/11. *Ethnic and Racial Studies*, 37(13), 2303–2321.

Sayyid, S. (2010). Out of the devil's dictionary. In S. Sayyid and A.K. Vakil (Eds.), *Thinking through Islamophobia: Global perspectives*(pp.1-18). Hurst.

Sayyid, S., & Vakil, A. (2010). *Thinking through Islamophobia: Global perspectives*. Hurst.

Schmidt, G. (2011). Understanding and approaching Muslim visibilities: Lessons learned from a fieldwork-based study of Muslims in Copenhagen. *Ethnic and Racial Studies*, 34(7), 1216–1229.

Scott, J. W. (2009). *The politics of the veil*. Princeton University Press.

Sharify-Funk, M. (2010). Muslims and the politics of "reasonable accommodation": Analyzing the Bouchard-Taylor report and its impact on the Canadian province of Quebec. *Journal of Muslim Minority Affairs*, 30(4), 535–553.

Shortell, T., & Brown, E. (2016). *Walking in the European city: Quotidian mobility and urban ethnography*. Routledge.

Simmel, G. (1997). *Simmel on culture: Selected writings* (Vol. 903). Sage Publications Ltd.

Sørensen, J. (2015, February 8). *Flere flytter fra landet til byerne [More people are moving from the countryside to the cities]*. DR. https://www.dr.dk/ligetil/indland/flere-flytter-fra-landet-til-byerne (Accessed: 13/10/2023).

Thisted, K. (2018). 'En gift i blodet': Følelsesøkonomier i de dansk-grønlandske relationer ['A poison in the blood': Economies of emotion in Danish-Greenlandic relations]. *K&K-Kultur Og Klasse*, 46(125), 71–94.

Tonnies, F., & Loomis, C. P. (2002). *Community and society*. Courier Corporation.

Times Out. (2021). *Time Out reveals the World's Coolest Neighbourhoods right now*. (Accessed: 13/10/2023) https://www.timeout.com/about/latest-news/time-out-reveals-the-worlds-coolest-neighbourhoods-right-now-100621

Urry, J. (2007). *Mobilities*. Polity.

Valluvan, S. (2019). *The clamour of nationalism: Race and nation in twenty-first-century Britain*. Manchester University Press.

Vigh, H. (2009). Motion squared: A second look at the concept of social navigation. *Anthropological Theory*, 9(4), 419–438.

Weheliye, A. G. (2014). *Habeas viscus: Racializing assemblages, biopolitics, and Black feminist theories of the human*. Duke University Press.

Vilhelmsen, A.(2013).*Et spørgsmål om ære* [A Question of Honour] Opinionen. http://opinionen.dk/debat/et-spoergsmaal-om-aere (access date: 27/02/2014).

Wekker, G. (2016). *White innocence: Paradoxes of colonialism and race*. Duke University Press.

Wren, K. (2001). Cultural racism: Something rotten in the state of Denmark? *Social & Cultural Geography*, 2(2), 141–162.

Yilmaz, F. (2016). *How the workers became Muslims: Immigration, culture, and hegemonic transformation in Europe*. University of Michigan Press.

Younis, T. (2023). *The Muslim, state and mind*. SAGE Publications.

Younis, T., & Jadhav, S. (2020). Islamophobia in the National Health Service: An ethnography of institutional racism in PREVENT's counter-radicalisation policy. *Sociology of Health & Illness*, 42(3), 610–626.

Index

abaya 93
abstract liberalism 2
Abu-Lughod, Lila 9–10, 59
agency 9–10, 12, 24, 73, 150; spatial agency 102
Al-Shamasnah, Fatima 51
Amit, Vered 62, 102–103, 107, 135–136, 145
Anderson, Elijah 80–81, 87
Anglophone imperialism 5
assemblages: racialisation 27–30; racialisation processes 24–27; space 30–34
assimilationist 40–41, 43
Assistentens Kirkegård 83, 95
assumed-to-be Muslim Other 30
at-risk 54

becoming, process of 142
belonging 11, 36–37, 50, 54–56, 148, 151
benevolent welfare state 6
Benhadjoudja, Leila 8
Bilge, Sirma 8
Bill 21 (prohibiting wearing of hijabs), Quebec 4, 58
Bill 60, "Charter of Values" 32–33
Bill 62, Quebec 58
Bill 94, Quebec 64
Bissonette, Alexandre 58
Black Baptist women's activism 41
Blågårdsplads 87–91
Blue Hijab event 70, 72–73
Bonilla-Silva, Eduardo 2–4, 6
Bouchard, Gérard 64
Bourchard/Taylor commission 64–65
Brubaker, Rogers 60, 62, 72–73, 150

Canada, belonging 36–37
cartographies of racialization 18, 150
cartoon crisis 37, 55

challenging social perceptions 82–87
"Charter of Values" (Bill 60) 32–33, 59–61, 70–71
chess, tactic for social mobility 52–54
childhood neighborhoods, as part of family history, Montreal 108–115
citizenship ceremony, Denmark 28
city spaces 81; creating self-image through 87–96
clothing 92
colour blindness 2
colour-blind societies 18–19, 24, 35, 149
community, Quebec 60–62
community gardens, Montreal 109–110
comparative ethnography 15, 135, 149
constructing, spatial biographies 106–108
constructing affluent self-image 82–87
Consultation Commission on Accommodation Practices Related to Cultural Differences 64
conviviality 81, 114
Copenhagen 16–17; challenging social perceptions 82–87; Nørrebro *see* Nørrebro; public iftar 33–34; self-image through city spaces 87–96; socioeconomic disparity 77; socioeconomic factors 77–78; "the yellow wall" 96–101; *see also* Denmark
Côte-des-Neiges (CDN), Montreal 116–123
Couillard, Philippe 58
counter-terrorism policies, United Kingdom 3
creativity 102
Crenshaw, Kimberlé 10, 26, 31
cultural anxiety 5, 37
cultural communities 7
cultural conformity 45

Index 161

cultural creativity 102
cultural differences 64
cultural inferiority 31
cultural racism 2–3
cultural war 37
culture 3

Danish community 38–39
Danish homogeneity, illusion of 36–39
Danish Muslims 50, 81; gendered
  perspectives 51–52; lifestyles
  48–49; as non-Westerners 42–43;
  respectability 42
Danish People's Party 36
Danish values 38
Danishness 45, 49–50
Dazey, Margot 41
De Certeau, Michel 14, 137–139, 151
Delueze, Gilles 25
democracy 5
Denmark 2; citizenship ceremony 28;
  discrimination 46–47; gentrification
  policies 84; illusion of homogeneity
  36–39; immigrants 37–38, 44–45,
  50–51; racialisation 39–41; racialised
  differentiation 6; representing
  internationally 54–56; shaking hands
  27–28; social mobility 52–54; welfare
  model 37; *see also* Copenhagen
differences 45, 71–73
discrimination: in Denmark 46–47;
  against Muslim women's dress
  58–59
diversity, Quebec 64
double consciousness 11
Drainville, Bernard 65
Du Bois, WEB 11

Elmegade, Nørrebro 91–92
El Tayeb, Fatima 3
erasure of race 5
ethnic 3
"ethnic Other" 96
ethnicity 3
ethnographic tools, urban walks 15–16
European racial denial 3
everyday life, experiencing racialisation
  43–46
exclusion, experiencing 46–51

Fadil, Nadia 6–7
family connections with religious
  community, Montreal 127–132

family history narrated through a
  childhood neighborhood, Montreal
  108–115
Finnegan, Ruth 136–137
foreignness 47, 93
frames of colour blindness 2–3
Frederiksen, Mette 38, 40
French Quebeckers 62–63
future, spatial biographies 139–141

Garner, Steve 8, 62
gender equality 4, 31; shaking hands
  27–28
gendered perspectives, Danish Muslims
  51–52
gentrification policies, Denmark 84
German Nazism 5
ghetto laws 84
Ghumkor, Sahar 59
Gilroy, Paul 5, 7, 81
Goldberg, David T. 3
Gould, Jørgen 50
grocery stores, Blågårdsplads 90
groupism 62
groupness 60–62, 72–73, 150
guest worker scheme, Denmark 43
Guettari, Félix 25

Habib, Sadia 11
Hallam, Elizabeth 102
Hamad Bin Khalifa Mosque 96–97
Hammoude, Jinan 51
Hannerz, Ulf 17
Higginbotham, Evelyn Brooks 41, 54
high culture 84–85
hijabs 58–60, 92; "Charter of Values"
  (Bill 60) 32–33; Islamic Awareness
  Week 32–33; as lack of integration
  47; oppressed Muslim women 29;
  prohibiting wearing of, Quebec
  58, 63; protest in Quebec 60–61;
  racialisation 27–30; representatives
  of Islam 68–69; as self-identification
  70–71
homogeneity, illusion of (Denmark)
  36–39
Hotel D'Angleterre 86

identity, through clothing 92
identity politics 65–66
illusion of, Danish homogeneity 36–39
immigrants: in Denmark 37–38, 44–45,
  50–51; in Quebec 65–66

162   *Index*

imperialism 2
improvisation in relation to mobility 102
Ingold, Tim 102
integration 36, 37; paradigm 50; policies 56, 64; process 12
interconnectedness, racialisation processes and spatialisation 30–34
interculturalism 6, 64, 65
intersectionality 26
invading spaces 99
invisibilising the Other 58
Islam, representatives of 66–69
Islamic Awareness Week 32–33
Islamophobia 5, 7–10, 38–39, 72

Jadhav, Shusrut 3
jazz 85n5

Kaffehuset 82–83, 93–94
Knowles, Caroline 13, 33, 79, 102–103, 107, 135–136, 145
Kongens Nytorv 85

Lefebvre, Henri 30, 101, 102, 151
Lentin, Alana 3
liberal nationalism 5
liberalism 4
Liep, John 102
lived space 138; *see also* space
localities 141–142

Mahmood, Saba 9–10, 32, 42, 73, 150
Mamdani, Mahmood 40
maps of Copenhagen 77–78
Marois, Pauline 65
Massey, Doreen 30
meaning-making processes, mobility and movements 143–146
memory, spatial biographies 136
middle class 4, 8–11, 18, 40–42, 57, 81, 84, 86, 100, 114, 124, 127, 150
middle-classness 4
migration 143
Mikkelsen, Brian 48–49
minimisation of racism 3
mobility 12–14; meaning-making processes 143–146; spatial mobility 135–136; transnational mobility 142; urban pathways 135–137; *see also* social mobility
Mondon, Aurelien 4–5, 58
Montreal 16–17, 109–110; family connections with religious community

127–132; family history narrated through a childhood neighborhood 108–115; Islamic Awareness Week 32–33; multicultural neighborhoods 116–123; suburban immigrant neighborhood 124–127; *see also* Quebec
mosque shooting, Quebec 58
movements, meaning-making processes 143–146
multicultural neighborhoods, Montreal 116–123
multiculturalism 65
Muslim belonging 151
Muslim community 36, 59, 62, 74
Muslim Copenhageners 94
Muslim minority 15
Muslim Other 5–6, 68, 82
Muslim Othering 13
"Muslim Question" 1
Muslim subjectivity 8
Muslim women: discrimination based on dress 58–59; hijabs 59–60; stereotypes 28–29, 60–61, 69, 71
Muslimness 1, 8, 11, 46, 148, 150; hijabs 59–60; respectability 40–42

national identification 66
nationalism 5, 7; Quebec 62–66
naturalisation 2
navigation: as mobility approach 12–14; spatial narratives 101–103; of urban spaces 106–108
Nazi-islamism 31–32
negotiating social position 43–56
The Netherlands 6
"new Danes" 45, 90
niqabs 58–59; racialisation 27–30
non-Westerners 77, 90–91; Danish Muslims 42–43
Nørrebro 79, 84; Blågårdsplads 87–91; *Kaffehuset* 82–83
nostalgia 139

official languages, Quebec 65
Old Pointe Claire Village, West Island, Montreal 145–146
oppressed Muslim women 28–29, 69, 71
Other, invisibilising 58
"other ethnic background" 90
Otherisation 11, 44
otherness 50

Parizeau, Jacques 63
Parti Québécois (PQ) 65
participants, urban ethnographic methods 15
pathways 136
Pedersen, Marianne Holm 37, 56
political discourse 25
political legitimacy 32
political nationalist narratives 5
politics of respectability 41–42
power dynamics 40; in assemblages 25–26; Muslim women's dress 59
prayer space 66–67
prejudice 39
Puar, Jasbir 25–26
public iftar 33–34
public representation, as self-identification 69–71
Puwar, Nirmal 34, 99–100

Quebec 2; Bill 21 4, 58; Bill 62 58; Bill 94 64; community 60–62; diversity 64; groupness 60–62; hijabs 63; immigrants 65–66; mosque shooting 58; Muslim community 59; nationalism 62–66; official languages 65; racialized differentiation 7; reasonable accommodations 62–66; religious symbols 65–66; representatives of Islam 66–69; self-identification 69–71; *see also* Montreal
Quiet Revolution 62–63

race 3, 6, 23; erasure of 5; space 33–35
racial denial 3
racialisation 8–9, 77, 149–150; assemblages 24–30; in Denmark 39–41; experiencing in everyday life 43–46; of Muslim men 100; of Muslim Other 6
racialisation processes 23–27; spatialisation and 30–34
racialized: differentiation, Denmark 6–7; hierarchy 7; Other 1, 30, 33–34, 43; social systems 4, 7–9
racializing: Muslim Others 23; Muslims 25
racism 5, 72; racialised social systems 4
racism/Islamophobia, liberalism 5; *see also* Islamophobia
racist tropes 39–40
Rasmussen, Anders Fogh 37, 48

reasonable accommodations, Quebec 62–66
religious communities, family connections with, Montreal 127–132
religious groupness 36
religious identification 12
religious symbols 59, 65–66
representation 36–37, 45, 148; categorical representations 51; community representation 60; counter-representation 72; ethnographic representation 16, 144, 147; hegemonic representation 84, 96; hijbas 47, 59; of Islam 66–69; media representation 63, 101; negative representation 55; political representations 50; public representation 69–71, 74, 142, 150; racialized representation 96, 101, 103, 140; self-representation 11, 14, 17, 56, 80, 82, 134, 138, 147, 149–150; social representation 13, 140, 151; spatial representation 94–96, 102–103, 134–135, 151
representational discourse 36
representatives of Islam 66–69
representing Denmark internationally 54–56
resistance 10
respectability 40–41
respectability politics 41–42
rootedness 105–106, 113; family history narrated through a childhood neighborhood 108–116; suburban immigrant neighborhood 124–127; through family connections with a religious community 127–132; walk through multicultural neighborhood 116–123
Royal Theatre 85
rural-urban migration 143
Rytter, Mikkel 37, 56

Scott, Joan 59
secularism 8; *laïcité* 65; secularity 32
securitisation 36; paradigm 37; policies 3, 56
self-ascription 8
self-identification 12, 69–71
self-image: constructing affluent self-image 82–87; creating through city spaces 87–96
Selod, Saher 8, 62

164   *Index*

separatist nationalist movement, Quebec 62–63
settlement, walk through multicultural neighborhood, Montreal 116–123
shaking hands 27–28
Simmel, Georg 106–107
social capital 100
social cohesion 38
social control 47
social mobility 12–13, 43, 52–54, 79–81, 99–100, 102–103, 108–115, 125–127
social navigation 144
social perceptions, challenging 82–87
social position 79–80; negotiation 43–56
socioeconomic factors 77
socioeconomic map of Copenhagen 78
socioeconomic mobility 4
space 135; assemblages 30–34; city spaces 81, 87–96; invading 99; race and 33–35; as text 79–80; urban spaces 106–108; White space 80–81
space invaders 99
spatial agency 102
spatial biographies 145; constructing 106–108; temporalities of 139–141; *see also* spatial narratives
spatial mobility 13, 135–136
spatial narratives 13–14, 107–108; Adam's tour 124–127; Amy's tour 116–123; as creative navigation 101–103; Dania's tour 87–96; Khadija's tour 82–87; Khalid's tour 96–101; Lisa's tour 145–146; Sidra's tour 108–115; subjectivity through 141–143; tactics of 137–139; temporalities of 139–141; Yaqub's tour 127–132
spatialization: racialisation processes and 30–34; of socioeconomic position 77–78
St. Joseph Oratory, Montreal 117–118
stereotypes 51–52; oppressed Muslim women 28–29, 60–61, 69, 71; submissiveness 52; "violent Muslim men" 27–28, 39–40
Støjberg, Inger 28

subjectivity in spatial accounts 141–143
subordination 11
suburban immigrant neighborhood, Montreal 124–127
symbolic gestures, shaking hands 27–28

tactics of spatial narratives 14, 137–139
Taylor, Charles 64
temporalities of spatial biographies 139–141
text, space as 79–80
time *see* space
transnational mobility 142
Trudeau, Pierre 64
"Try on hijab" stand, Islamic Awareness Week 33

United Kingdom, counter-terrorism policies 3
urban ethnographic methods 15
urban life 89, 95, 117, 118, 136
urban pathways 135–137
urban spaces, navigating 106–108
urban walks 15–16
Urry, John 12–13, 135
"us vs them" 43, 45, 48, 151

Valluvan, Sivamohan 3
Vigh, Henrik 14, 144
Vilhelmsen, Anette 47
"violent Muslim men" 27–28, 39–40

"walkabout" 134
War on Terror 1, 3, 30, 40
Weheliye, Alexander G. 25–26
Wekker, Gloria 6
welfare model, Denmark 37
West Island, Montreal 124–130, 132
white segregation 2
White space 80–81
white spaces 15
Winter, Aaron 4–5, 58
"the yellow wall" 80, 83, 95; growing up on the other side of 96–101

Yilmaz, Ferruh 7, 8, 51
Younis, Tarek 3, 8–9

Printed in the United States
by Baker & Taylor Publisher Services